C000259257

A LIFE

IS

WHAT YOU GET

Lynn M. Trowbridge

Read Fox Books

Fourth Edition published in 2016
by
Read Fox Books

All rights reserved © Lynn M. Trowbridge 2015

No part of this publication may be reproduced, stored in
a retrieval system, or transmitted in any form or any
means, electronic, mechanical, photocopy, recording or
otherwise without prior written consent from the
copyright holder.

The rights of Lynn Trowbridge to be identified as author
of this work has been asserted in accordance with
Section 77 of the Copyright, Designs and Patents Act
1988

ISBN 978-0-9932564-0-0

Distributed by the author, 6,Harley Almshouses,
Hay-on-Wye, Hereford HR3 5DZ
Email: l.trowbridge23@btinternet.com

Printed in the United Kingdom
By Powerprint,
Oxford Chambers, High Street,
Llandrindod Wells, Powys, LD1 6AG

ACKNOWLEDGEMENTS

My grateful thanks to my friends for their kindness and support throughout the writing of this book: Lyn Webster Wilde, who first encouraged me in the belief that I could do it. Alex James who did the initial proof reading and inspired me to carry on, and to my good friend Clare Cross who has proof read, helped me with certain technical aspects of getting into print; co-selected which photographs to use, and who has had the patience and endurance to stick by me throughout all the arguments and my occasional petulant strops.

Without the help and encouragement of these and other friends, this book may well have remained an unfulfilled dream.

Chapter 1

1980s

I sat at the head of the dining table with a company director on each side of me and my staff arrayed down either side of the long dining table. It was a celebration of my twenty-five years with the company and I was duly presented with the statuary gold watch that marked such occasions. The wine flowed, the conversation was easy, and in my speech I gave credit to the staff, and graciously acknowledged their contribution to my success and the success of the Branch that I managed. I then thanked my directors for their faith in appointing me the first and only lady Branch Manager in the Company and said how grateful I was to have been given the opportunity to prove that a woman could succeed in what had essentially been a man's world. Then, flushed with pride, I sat down to a round of enthusiastic applause and beamed magnanimously on anyone who happened to catch my attention.

The waitress at our end of the table was very attentive, a bit too much so I felt, for each time she attended my needs she would turn her head and look right into my face. I began to wonder if she thought I was some sort of celebrity or other, or worse. Perhaps there was a smut on the end of my nose, which wouldn't do at all; so just in case, I surreptitiously dabbed at it to be on the safe side.

The people around me were hanging on my every word as I entertained them with some amusing anecdotes, and I felt I was truly living up to the image I had of myself, as an astute, successful and sophisticated business woman.

After the last course the over-familiar waitress appeared again to serve the coffee.

'Black or white?' she enquired

'White please,' I said, and lidded my eyes to avoid her intrusive stare. She poured the coffee. I raised my eyes to say 'Thank you' only to see she was scrutinising my face once more.

'Excuse me,' she said. 'Ain't you one of the 'ome girls?'

I ignored the question as if I hadn't heard it and hoped no one else had. Although I didn't recognise her, I guessed she was probably about the same age as me – fifties - and had most likely attended the same elementary school in Leamington that I had. We girls from St. Anne's were easily identifiable from the other children by the type of clothing we wore and were often referred to (not unkindly) by the other pupils as *The Home Girls*.

I thought I had successfully shed the old garments of my closely guarded, inauspicious beginnings, but this unexpected and embarrassing reminder got me thinking about my past; why I never spoke of it and was it *really* something of which I should be ashamed.

Chapter 2

1920s

Amongst my earliest childhood memories was attending Sunday School in the 1920's. Most people in the little South Wales mining village where I belonged attended some form of worship on a Sunday and our family was no exception.

We always wore our Sunday best clothes, which were never worn on a week-day until they were past their best or getting too small. Then, and then only, were they relegated to everyday wear and never worn on Sundays again. This was an unspoken law obeyed by all.

Whit Sunday was always a special occasion. This was the time when all we children were decked out in our new summer finery. We would assemble outside our various places of worship, then proudly march along the streets singing *Onward Christian Soldiers* or *Forward be Our Watchword* and other stirring hymns, finally ending up at our respective church halls where we received our Sunday School prizes and were treated to iced buns, cakes, sandwiches and lemonade or tea. Having had, and still have an appalling sense of direction, on one of these occasions I somehow managed to get lost and ended up in the wrong church hall. By the time I found my way back to where I was supposed to be, the prize giving was over, nearly all the food eaten, I'd missed the prize giving and I was swooped on by my frantic mother who roundly scolded me for getting lost then hugged me for being found.

My mother sang in the church choir. For a time I was worried about her, as, unlike the other choir members, she did not appear to shine. I thought all true Christians shone and would sometimes give my forehead a crafty rub on the way to Sunday School in the hope it would make me look shiny and good. It was a long time before I realised that she didn't shine because she wore make-up, and then I worried in case she might be thought of as something of a Jezebel.

I think my pre-occupation with shining may have started when, at the age of about four or five, I was coached to sing solo, the verse:

> *Jesus bids me shine with a pure clear light,*
> *Like a little candle, burning in the night.*
> *In this world of darkness, so we must shine,*
> *You in your small corner and I in mine.*

When the time came for me to sing, I remember my mother anxiously mouthing the words and nodding her head in time, which gave me the confidence to sing with all the fervour of a budding prima donna. When I finished, she turned her head slightly towards the people either side of her and smiled a lip-closed, proud smile.

I glanced at Mr. Morgan, the organist and choirmaster (or Morgan the Organ as he was more popularly known) in the expectation of a congratulatory smile, or at least a nod of approval. None came, not even a glance in my direction, so occupied was he with his organ playing. I kept my eye on him anyway – just in case.

On Sundays he always wore a black, pinstripe suit with a flower in the lapel on one side of his jacket and a white handkerchief in the pocket of the other side. He was a small, wizened man, with black, crinkly hair, sharp features and wore pince-nez glasses on the end of his nose. He had a hump on his back and looked a bit like a wizard. When it was time for the sermon he settled himself down in a pew near the organ. I continued to glance at him from time to time in the hope of catching his eye but he would not look at me and I began to get fidgety and bored. Then, suddenly my attention was riveted. Wide-eyed, I watched as he removed the large, pristine white

4

handkerchief from his breast pocket and shook it out with a great flourish. Next, he took a long, sharply honed pencil from another part of his person and held it, point upwards, between the thumb and finger of his left hand.

My eyes grew wide with eager anticipation. A conjuring trick it is, especially for me. With a further flourish, he dropped the handkerchief over the pencil and deftly twirled it until it was neatly wrapped around. With mounting excitement I waited for the magic trick. My disappointment knew no bounds when he then calmly and unashamedly cleaned out his ears.

Chapter 3

I was six years old when my sister Muriel was born and I was not pleased. For a while I showed no interest in her at all and I'm sure, if I'd had the opportunity, I might have done her a mischief. But my resentment and ill intent didn't last and after a spell of pretending that I loved her, I eventually got to really love her. But this didn't stop me, when she was a bit older, carrying out sneaky, experimental tricks on her; as when I tied one end of a long rope to a tree in the garden and tied the other end round her waist, then told her to run as hard as she could. Another time, I cut her hair thinking it would make it curly like mine and was horrified when I saw the result of my first incursion with the scissors. I threatened her, on pain of death, not to say who'd done it and she didn't, but eventually I became so over-whelmed with guilt that I confessed, dramatically throwing myself on the floor and crying out, 'You know you wanted to know who cut Muriel's hair. Well, it was me…sob…sob…' Whether I was punished or not has escaped my memory, but it was punishment enough to see how odd Muriel looked when all I'd intended was to make her look pretty.

I didn't go to dancing classes as most little girls would want to but joined a local gymnastic club. We put on displays in a big hall which served variously as a concert venue, a cinema, meeting place for the Band of Hope, for boxing and wrestling matches and other forms of entertainment.

A lady once visited our club whose claim to fame was that she was the strongest woman in the world. We practised for a gymnastic performance in the Big Hall and one of the things she did to demonstrate her prodigious strength was to stand, legs apart and slightly bent and support a pyramid of seven

6

people precariously placed on various parts of her anatomy. I was the only child in this display and my part was to be neatly handed up, one over the other, until I stood, one footed, leaning forward with arms outstretched to the side, on the head of the man who was standing on her shoulders. My desire to perform obviously overcame my fear.

Another proof of her strength was for her to stand on a raised dais, have a man in some sort of harness in front of her with his back to her and she would then raise him from the ground clutching the harness in her teeth. I was impressed and secretly nurtured the thought that I might one day become the strongest woman in the world. To this end, I used to practice this feat of strength on my long suffering little sister. Having no harness or platform I would sink my teeth into the back of the collar of whatever she was wearing, lift her off the ground (much as a cat might carry its kitten) and deposit her in another place. She used to cough a bit and go a funny colour but never complained or cried.

My ambition to become the strongest woman in the world quickly vanished when I started to go to the cinema on a Saturday morning, pocket money three pence a week, two pence to go in and a penny for sweets. Lovely it was sitting there, sucking the sweets and watching Shirley Temple sing and dance her way through *The Good Ship Lollipop*. Better than this though were the cowboy films. It was then that I resolved that when I grew up I would be a cowboy, although I hadn't quite worked out how I was going to make the transition from an ordinary little girl in a Welsh village to a swaggering, gun slinging, guitar playing young hero, crooning romantic songs such as *Roll Along Prairie Moon* and *When its Springtime in the Rockies* round a camp fire. But my dreams were not going to be spoiled by thinking too much about how they were to be achieved.

In the event, my ambition to become a cowboy was soon abandoned when I saw the film *The Scarlet Pimpernel*. So impressed was I with Sir Percy Blakeney's exploits in rescuing members of the French aristocracy during the French Revolution that I now decided I wanted to emulate his daring feats and become a female equivalent. Problem was, there were no more French aristocrats to be rescued, so I would have to dream up another worthy mission and adopt the name of another flower. After much thought, I decided to adopt the appellation of a little wild flower called the Star of Bethlehem and I would rescue the Jews, although at that time I wasn't aware they needed rescuing, or from whom they could be rescued.

Such were my enjoyable wild imaginings, which I could freely indulge whilst basking in the luxury of a cosy, trouble-free childhood. It was not to last. First my maternal grandmother, who was living with us at the time, became ill and died of yellow jaundice. It did not affect me much at the time, but I saw my mother crying and thought it would please her if she saw me crying too, so I followed her about and managed a few convincing sobs whenever I thought I'd got her attention. In the meantime, my father had had to give up working down the pit because of his bad lungs. This didn't worry me too much as there were lots of men with bad lungs who were out of work. In the summer they would sit in circles in the field that fronted the houses and play cards and chatter, grumble and cough. Often, when someone died, they would put on their Sunday suits and bowler hats and gather outside the house of the deceased and sing hymns like *The Old Rugged Cross* or *Jesu Lover of my Soul*. I often stopped to listen, not thinking about the dead person, or the grieving family, but just to listen to the lovely singing.

Chapter 4

The Last home.

We had a little grocery shop which, in theory, was now our main means of support. My mother was also a dressmaker which was another source of income. But eventually the shop had to close because now, with the coal mining strikes, unemployment, and general poverty, everyone seemed to obtain their goods *on tick* and then couldn't pay at the end of the week. Dad used to carry on and say they shouldn't be allowed any further credit until they paid, but Mam would argue, 'Let them have it – how can you let the little ones starve.'

I don't know quite when my mother first started to get ill but I was probably about eight or nine. I remember coming home from school one day, and finding the table already laid, sat down for my tea. But Mam wasn't there to greet me; my little sister wasn't anywhere to be seen and neither was my father, so I sat patiently at the table and waited – until I realised the table wasn't laid for tea – it hadn't been cleared from the last meal.

Hungry, disappointed and worried, I got out of my chair and started to clear the dirty dishes from the table and put them into the kitchen sink. I tried switching the gas cooker on to boil a kettle but the gas had run out and I hadn't any pennies to feed the meter. So I washed the dishes up, after a fashion, in cold water and continued to wait and worry. Mam would be ever so pleased, I thought, when she saw what I'd done. I looked at my exercise book languishing in the chair where I'd dumped it, but felt too anxious to tackle my homework, so it remained untouched. I went out into the street and looked up and down and it was then that I saw Mrs. Coles hurrying towards me. 'Come on my lovely,' she said. 'Tea is all ready and I've got Muriel with me.'

I followed Mrs. Coles hoping she was going to give me some of her lovely, white fluffy fruit cake, of which she always seemed to have a plentiful supply.

'Where's Mam and Dad? I asked.

'Don't you worry about that now. Just sit you down and have your tea. You'll have some bread and butter is it?'

I agreed I would, for I knew the white fluffy fruit cake would soon follow, but it didn't stop me worrying about where Mam and Dad had got to.

At last Dad turned up looking weary and worried and wheezing worse than ever. He accepted the proffered cup of tea and slice of bread and jam and thanked Mrs. Coles for taking care of us. All I could think of at that moment was: I hope he doesn't take us home before we get to eat the cake.

He didn't, but I nearly choked on the cake when I learned Mam had been taken to the T.B. Hospital at Cefn Mably, Cardiff. I recalled a snatch of over-heard conversation once when Mam collapsed in the backyard whilst pummelling the washing with a dolly stick. The doctor came and I was lurking outside the bedroom door when I heard her say: 'No doctor – I don't want to go to the Cefn Mably - that's your last home.'

I looked at Dad. He looked tired after his long walk to the hospital and back so I didn't question him about letting them take her to her *last home*. That evening I went to The Band of Hope meeting and prayed like I'd never prayed before or since. It made no difference – she died anyway.

At nine years old I knew that my childhood was virtually over. Gone were my childish fantasies and outrageous ambitions. I was now the mother to Muriel and housekeeper to my father but I don't think I made a very good job of it. With the shop gone, the income from Mam's dressmaking gone and Dad being too ill to work (even if there was any work to be had) we had to live off what was then known as Parish Relief, plus a small army pension Dad had because of his war wounds.

I did the housework, gathered wood from the woods, coal from the slag heaps and lit the fires and didn't think it too much of a hardship. Dad did the cooking, which I think consisted mainly of things like beans on toast, cheese on toast or tinned tomatoes on toast and we took cocoa powder mixed with sugar screwed up in a piece of newspaper to school for our mid-day meal. I don't remember doing any washing so I think Mrs. Coles might have done that.

Muriel and I stopped going to Sunday School as we no longer had any Sunday best to wear. The Vicar came to see us once or twice and told us what naughty girls we were for not going to church. I was too embarrassed to tell him why, so I said we hadn't got any collection money.

'Collection. Collection is it?' he said, 'well, don't you worry about that, just you come anyway.'

Despite all the problems at home, I was a bright pupil, always anxious to please and managed somehow to do my homework, although I became very withdrawn and kept myself to myself. I remember an occasion when one of the teaching staff – a Miss Morgan, tall, slim, beautifully dressed and always smelling of Lilies of the Valley, strode purposefully into the classroom bearing an armful of exercise books and fixed her stern gaze on me.

I shrank into my ragged clothes and put my arms under the desk so that she wouldn't see the shiny, snot-stiffened sleeves of my coat. Despite her sternness, I loved Miss Morgan and wanted her to love me, but I knew I was unworthy of any love she had to spare. Not because I was a naughty child – I wasn't – all I wanted was to be good, conform and please her. But I knew I was not a pleasing child with my dirty, uncared for appearance, clothes that were mostly unwashed and certainly too small, and my Parish Relief lace-up boots which I hated, but at least they hid the large holes in the heels of my socks. I blushed as I tried desperately to think what I could have done to

11

displease her. Her gaze left me and focussed on a child who was glancing at me and whispering and giggling. No need for words. Her stern stare was enough to silence even the most wilful child.

Then she began: 'Before we begin the next lesson I'm going to read you the best of the stories I set you for homework.

She read out three stories and I was disappointed mine was not amongst them. Then she stopped and fixed me with another of her unnerving stares.

'Those were very good indeed,' she said, 'but there is one that is better than all the rest. Lynn, would you come to the front and read your story to the class.'

'Yes Miss,' I said with mixed feelings - pleased that my story was the best, but embarrassed to be standing in front of the class, exposed in all my scruffiness.

Memory is a strange thing. I vividly recall the episode but have no recollection of what the story was about.

Chapter 5

Christmas 1933

Muriel had just had her fourth birthday at the beginning of November when she became very ill and was diagnosed with pneumonia. I stayed off school to help look after her and prayed and cried over her and promised her all manner of things if she would get better, even to the point of saying I would buy her a bicycle when I grew up. (I did not have to keep the promise as she never learned to ride a bike!)

We had a wind-up gramophone and amongst our meagre collection of records were some by Ernest Lough (a then famous boy soprano). Two of my favourites were *Oh for the Wings of a Dove* and *Hear my Prayer* and I played them over and over again.

Muriel had now pulled through the so-called 'crisis' in the cycle of pneumonia and survived, and I knew she was really getting better when I went into the bedroom and saw her sitting up trying to sing *O For the Wings of a Dove.*

I went back to school but I was now a long way behind the rest of the class and my exercise books no longer bulged with Gold Stars. So I would sit, miserable and frustrated because I found it difficult to catch up. When it was time to sort out the pupils for the *scholarship* class and I wasn't selected I was heartbroken, although I realised in later life that due to my circumstances I probably wouldn't have stood a chance of going to grammar school anyway, even if I had proved myself academically capable.

On Christmas Eve I sat at the table in the cheerless kitchen, chewing thoughtfully on the end of my pencil, trying to compose a letter to Father Christmas. I was now ten years old and wasn't sure I still believed in him, but I would keep up the pretence for Muriel's sake. I wrote the date: 24th December

1933 and got as far as *Dear Father Christmas* when my thoughts were interrupted by my father's rasping coughing, followed by hawking and spitting into the dying embers of the fire. I hated him doing this and wished he wouldn't, especially when the fire was barely hot enough to sizzle the phlegm. And I hated it even more now, for it wouldn't be very nice for Father Christmas, if he *was* going to visit, to come down the chimney and get his boots all gunged up.

I continued with the letter. *Dear Father Christmas, I'm sorry*...I chewed on my pencil some more trying to think how I could apologise for the messy grate without using indelicate words, but there was no polite way to say it, so rather than scratch out the beginning of the letter, I tried to think of something else to be sorry for.

Not for myself. No, I wasn't sorry for myself but I was sorry for Muriel, still recuperating from her illness. I was also sorry for my father, whose annoying cough had got worse and whom I knew instinctively, would die soon. And I was sorry we didn't really have enough to eat.

Ah yes – food. That's what I could be sorry about. So I continued: *Dear Father Christmas, I'm sorry we haven't got any mince pies or a drink of sherry for you this year...*

I looked up again as Dad's coughing once more impinged on my thoughts. 'Can I get you a drink of water Dad?' I asked, 'and shall I go and see if Muriel's all right?'

'No, no,' he wheezed. 'Just see to Muriel, there's a good girl.'

Muriel was still weak, but I was confident now that at least *she* wasn't going to die. I made her a meal of broken bread soaked in warm milk with a sprinkling of sugar and took it up to the bedroom. We ate it together – a spoonful each at a time – and when we had finished I thought to tell her a story. But before the story could be told we heard the sound of music. I went to the window and looked out. It was a crisp, star-studded night and under the street gas-lamp I could see the Salvation Army Band.

We listened, enraptured, as the band played the familiar carols: *While Shepherds Watched...It Came Upon a Midnight Clear...O Little Town of Bethlehem...* This last was my favourite carol. I knew all the words and sang them, Muriel joining in where she could, and I felt sad when it came to the verse:

> *Where children pure and happy,*
> *Pray to the blessed Child,*
> *Where misery cries out to Thee,*
> *Son of the mother mild;*
> *Where charity stands watching*
> *And faith holds wide the door,*
> *The dark night wakes, the glory breaks,*
> *And Christmas comes once more.*

The words reminded me of Christmases past, when Dad was working, Mam was still alive and we were all 'pure and happy.'

I was sorry when the band moved on, for I thought the music and the singing was lovely, and for a short while I felt uplifted and filled with hope and the magic of Christmas. I hung up an old sock for Muriel at the bottom of the bed and stayed with her until Dad put his head round the door and wheezed a sad 'goodnight.'

'Goodnight,' Dad, I said, with false cheerfulness. 'See you in the morning.'

I think he'd stopped hugging and kissing us in case he gave us his germs, not because he didn't like us anymore.

As soon as I thought he was settled in his bedroom I crept down the stairs to finish my letter to Father Christmas. Then I framed the edges of the paper with drawings of holly and ivy, folded it carefully, and now that the fire was out, placed the letter on a ledge part way up the chimney. Next, I went to the cupboard to retrieve the apple and orange I'd pinched off the greengrocer's cart and the chocolate Father Christmas I'd bought with the money I got from Mrs. Cohen for lighting her fire on a Saturday because her religion forbade her to do any form of work on the Jewish Sabbath. Then I looked in the drawer for the rag doll I'd tried to make, hiding its nakedness and imperfections by wrapping a treasured embroidered handkerchief round it. I crept back upstairs and quietly popped the presents into Muriel's hanging sock. Then, more in hope than expectation, I hung up a sock for myself.

The following morning I woke early and with faint optimism, went to the bottom of the bed to see if he'd *been*. He hadn't.

I went downstairs and felt up the chimney to where I'd put the letter – it was still there. I lit a candle and re-read the letter to make sure I hadn't said anything that could possibly have offended Santa:

Dear Father Christmas,

I'm sorry we couldn't leave you a mince pie and sherry this year so I don't think you'll leave us anything, but if you do could you leave a doll with some clothes for Muriel, and a packet of Woodbines for my Dad. You needn't leave me anything but if you do I'd like a torch.

Love from Lynn

I ripped the letter up, cross with myself for having forgotten to say 'please' and 'thank you'. Then I cleared out the grate and laid the fire, using the torn letter as part of the kindling. I knew now for sure... but I wouldn't tell. With a sad heart, I went back to bed to wait for Muriel to wake up.

'Has he been? Has he been? She murmured when she opened her eyes.

'Yes. I think he's been,' I lied. 'But I forgot to ask him for a proper doll, so I think he might have left you a rag one instead.'

Muriel examined the contents of her sock, bit the head off the chocolate Father Christmas, then asked me what I'd got.

'It's early, we'll look later,' I said. 'Let's coochie down for now and go back to sleep.'

I tried to think of something to make us feel happy and remembered the music and singing by the Salvation Army. 'Wasn't that music lovely last night', I whispered. Then I thought about Jesus – *Away in a manger, no crib for his bed* – and thought: 'At least we're in a proper bed in a proper house and not shivering in a draughty stable.'

Later that day Mr. Coles came to fetch us to share their Christmas dinner. After the meal Mrs. Coles handed us some wrapped presents and by some miracle or other Muriel got a proper doll, my present was a small electric torch and Dad had a packet of fags. So perhaps there really *was* a Father Christmas after all!

Chapter 6

Childish Crush

Christmas holidays over it was back to school. I took my torch and got in trouble for switching it on and off, so it was confiscated and I don't remember what happened to it after that. It was a pity because I found going outside to the toilet in the dark very scary and the torch was a great comfort.

There was a boy in my class called Billy Williams who sat behind me and on whom I'd developed a childish crush. He had lovely rosy cheeks, velvet brown eyes, dark curly hair and always looked well fed and cared for. I had no hope of my crush being reciprocated, but it was enough that he gave my tangled hair an occasional tug from behind and smiled cheekily if I turned round.

Despite my having missed a lot of school, he wasn't as bright as me, and couldn't get his sums right, so in response to a gentle poke in the back, my only way of expressing my secret admiration for him was to surreptitiously turn round and whisper the answers, until, that is, we were caught red-handed when we both had exactly the same mistakes. It wasn't proved who was copying from whom so we both got a caning. I never gave him the answers again, although I missed the hair tugging and the little pokes in the back. He never played with me in the playground anyway, so I knew he didn't like me as much as I liked him and this was just another early lesson in conditioning myself to deal with disappointment.

One day Dad said Granny Trowbridge was coming to stay with us as he might have to go away for a while. She lived a long way away and we didn't see her very often, so we didn't really know her all that well. The day after she arrived Dad disappeared and I discovered that he too had now been admitted to Cefn Mably Hospital. Granny was a slender

18

woman with a ramrod back and always wore a black, shiny material dress that reached almost to her ankles and buttoned right up to her neck.

She wore pointed black shoes that met her skirt and which fastened to the side and had to be done up with a button hook, which she couldn't always manage; so I sometimes knelt on the floor and buttoned them up for her.

She had steel grey hair scraped to the back of her head and secured in a bun and her face looked pale, pinched and careworn. She carried a white cane and I thought she'd brought it to hit us with. It took me some time to realise that she was almost blind – hence the stick.

It didn't take her long to introduce some proper organisation into the house, and although I willingly acquiesced with most of the new order of things, I think I might also have felt a little resentful that I was no longer *in charge.*

Chapter 7

A Change of Circumstances

I can't say I enjoyed her looking after us, although there was no one else to do it. Then, one day the Vicar paid us another visit. When I saw him coming my instinct was to hide so I wouldn't have to be reprimanded for not going to Sunday school again. So I went out into the back garden and left Granny to say whatever she wished about our non-attendance. But I hadn't been lurking outside for long before I was called indoors.

'The Vicar has something to say to you,' said Granny.

I shot him a half- resentful, half-ashamed look before he began..

'How would you and your sister like to go to a Children's Home in Leamington Spa?'

I brightened. 'Would it be like a girls boarding school? I asked..

'Yes – just like it,' he replied.

I'd read a lot of Eleanor M. Brent-Dyer's books about girls boarding schools and for a long time had wished I could go to one. Now here was my God given chance.

'Yes. I'd like that very much,' I said. Then added, 'and I think Muriel would like it too.'

I had no idea where Leamington Spa was, but it sounded grand and I discovered from my geography book that it was in Warwickshire and not far from Kenilworth. This was an added incentive as I'd recently read Walter Scott's historical novel called *Kenilworth* and I was excited at the thought that I might actually get to see the castle sometime.

The day soon came for our departure. Granny had somehow scraped enough money together to buy me a new coat and as

Muriel hadn't grown much, the coat my mother had made for her still fitted quite nicely.

I was too excited for tearful farewells and felt as if we were embarking on a great adventure. The vicar travelled with us on the short train journey to Newport, where we were then put on a train which would take us to Leamington Spa.

In the carriage we sat near a nice, friendly lady who engaged us in conversation. She asked where we were going, how old we were and why were we travelling alone. I told her we were going to a Children's Home in Leamington, that my name was Lynn and my sister's name was Muriel and that she was four and I was ten. We were on our own because there was no one to travel with us. The nice lady gave us some chocolate, then lifted Muriel onto her lap and cuddled her until the end of our journey. I looked out of the window and marvelled at the changing scenery. I'd never travelled more than about twenty miles from home before and that was when, in better times, we went on the Sunday School outing on the charabanc to Barry Island. But this was something altogether more exciting and life changing.

Chapter 8

New Beginnings

When we reached Leamington the nice lady pressed a sixpenny piece each into our hands and gave us a quick hug before we took the terrifyingly steep steps from the train to the platform to start a new chapter in our young lives. We waved the lady and the train off and then I had a few moments panic wondering how we were to find our way to St. Anne's Home. My bewilderment quickly dissolved when an imposing, yet kindly looking elderly lady emerged from the throng of people on the platform and led us out to her car. I learned later that she was a member of the Home committee.

As we drove through the tree lined avenues, the town centre with its magnificent shops, glimpsed the beautiful municipal gardens and passed huge houses with their own individual drives, I realised Leamington Spa was every bit as grand as its posh sounding name had suggested it might be. I whispered to Muriel, whilst munching on the apple Mrs. Glover had given us, 'I think we'll like it here.'

We reached the outskirts of the town, where the stucco fronted houses with their large gardens, semi-circular driveways and imposing iron gates were even more impressive than I could ever have imagined and eventually, the car swept into the drive of just such a house. We followed the lady up the wide stone steps that led to an enormous front door. She gave a light tug on an iron knob to the right of the door frame, which set a bell jangling. We waited a few moments and as no one came she raised her hand to pull again.

'Can I pull it please?' I said excitedly.

We changed positions so I could reach and just as I pulled, the door was opened by a very cross looking woman, who glared at Muriel and I, before exchanging a few pleasantries with the nice lady, who then promptly disappeared. I don't recall any friendly greeting or any attempt being made to make us feel welcome. We were handed over to someone who didn't look quite so forbidding as the person we originally encountered, and taken to the bathroom. We were told to remove our clothes, which were taken away, including my new coat. Our hair was washed in some awful smelling concoction, then scraped with a fine tooth comb, after which we were told to get into the baths. The only bath we'd ever been in before was a tin one, in the kitchen, so this was a new experience, and whilst I enjoyed it, poor Muriel was terrified. I felt sorry for her but was also a bit cross as I wanted them to think we were quite used to bathing in this sort of manner and not a tin bath in front of the kitchen fire. She was lifted up and after much screaming and kicking of her little legs she was lowered into the bath, but I think in the end she also enjoyed the experience.

Next we were taken to another part of the house and fitted out with our "Home" uniform. Understandably, the clothes were all second hand and I didn't mind this. They were better than what we had (apart from my new coat) and I would have been very pleased to have them but for the fact that the gym slip I'd been given, instead of being a smart navy blue, had gone purple with age and the pleats had been 'bottomed out' at the back. But it was the only one that fitted and I wore it for at least two years. The underwear was a bit strange. We were given an all in one woollen garment known as "combinations" which, as the name suggested, served as knickers and vest all in one.

When it was time for bed I was dismayed that Muriel was put into a different dormitory from me. What if she wanted to go to the toilet in the night – how would she know where to go. I'd been shown a row of toilets on the ground floor at the back of the huge house, but how on earth would we find our way there in the night?

I got into the nice, clean little bed allocated to me, pulled the bedclothes over my head and started to snivel. I cried for Muriel and I cried for my father. What would happen if he came out of hospital and discovered we weren't at home anymore. How would he know where to find us. Then I remembered Mam saying Cefn Mably was your *last home* so I thought he would die anyway - not knowing where we were, which made me cry even more.

The girl in the bed next to me asked me why I was crying and I told her I was worried about my father who was in hospital.

'Don't worry,' she whispered, 'God will take care of him.'

I didn't answer her but thought to myself: That's what *you* think - you don't know Him like I do. Even so, I uttered a silent prayer: '*Please God don't let Dad die and don't let Muriel wet the bed.'* The following day did not start well. Muriel *did* wet the bed and got a smacking. We all sat down at our allocated table places and were served porridge for breakfast. It was sugarless, thick and stodgy, but I was starving and ate mine up without any trouble. But I could see that Muriel, who was on another table was struggling with hers and eventually gave up on it. When it was time to leave the table one of the staff went over to her and started to shovel the porridge into her mouth, but the more she shovelled the more Muriel heaved and protested and I could only watch, sorry and helpless.

I was relieved when it was time to line up and walk, crocodile fashion, to the local elementary school about half a mile away. Her ordeal was over and at least we were walking together and I could hold her hand and comfort her.

After an interview with the headmaster we were placed in classes presumably commensurate with our ages and level of intelligence, but I don't remember much about that first day of lessons. The thing that sticks in my mind was when we got back to the Home for lunch. It was mashed potato with boiled fish covered in revolting black skin. I carefully removed the skin and pushed it to the side of my plate, then ate the fish and potato and placed my knife and fork in the middle of the plate to indicate that I'd finished. I looked across to the table where Muriel was sitting to see how she was getting on, and realised that instead of the meal we were having, the porridge had been put in front of her again. I watched helplessly as she toyed with the now cold, stodgy mess and I bit my lips and blinked to stop myself crying on her behalf, but to my great relief, she finally managed to get it all down.

A bell was rung to signal it was time for the dirty dishes to be passed along to the end of the table. As I was on the end, I piled all the plates on top of mine in the hope that my leavings would be hidden. Not a bit of it! On their way out of the dining room one of the hawk-eyed staff noticed the black skin hanging over the edge of the plate.

'Whose plate is that?' she demanded, and I admitted it was mine.

'We can't afford to waste good food here,' she snarled, whereupon, the pile of plates were lifted from mine and I was told to finish my meal. Despite Muriel's experience with the porridge, I couldn't believe that anyone would be expected to eat black skin, especially as it had had a pile of dirty plates plonked on top of it, but I already guessed that to protest would be futile, so I swallowed it in two gulps without chewing, then rushed to the toilets and threw up.

I'd had my first lesson in not leaving any food on my plate and thereafter secreted anything not to my liking up my elasticated knicker-leg. I told Muriel to do the same but stodgy porridge was hardly knicker-leg material, and it broke my heart each morning to watch from a distance as she heaved her way through the sugarless stodge, sitting alone at what was known as the 'piggy-table'.

It was on returning from school on that first day that I hesitated outside the gates to the Home to read the sign emblazoned large on one of the portals. It read:

St. Anne's Church of England Home

for

Waifs & Strays.

I puzzled about this for I didn't quite know what a 'waif' was, and I thought it was only cats and dogs that were 'strays' so I made so bold as to say to one of the staff, 'Please Miss, what's a waif and stray? '

It was a mistake, for she bit my head off and said, 'That's what you are.'

Lesson two: we weren't ordinary children anymore – we were waifs and strays.

And so ended the first day of our new life.

Chapter 9

Life at St. Anne's

I soon realised the person who opened the front door to us on our arrival was in charge of the Home and was to be addressed as Matron. A smallish, neatly compacted woman, she wore a close fitting grey uniform. Her hair was crisp and iron grey, her eyes were hard and steely grey and her complexion was a papery pale grey without a relieving hint of pink, except when she was angry (which I discovered was quite often) and then she would go red. Her tight, cruel lips, were also a sort of mauvish grey. Everything was grey except for her black shoes and stockings and the white veil she wore over her head, which made her seem even more intimidating.

There were three other members of staff dressed in ordinary clothes whom we were to address as 'Miss' usually followed by their surname. They seemed much more approachable and looking back, were probably almost as much in fear of Matron Calcutt as we children were. Miss Clifford, at age probably about twenty, was much younger than the other members of staff and much kinder and I often saw her shedding a tear when one or the other of the children was being severely punished for some real or trumped up misdemeanour.

As is the case with children, we soon got used to the routine and discipline of our new life and, although at times it was harsh and unloving, at least our physical needs were taken care of. We had clean, bug free beds, clean clothes for school, and, what was most important to me at the time, special clothes for Sunday. We had regular meals, meagre and unappetizing though most of them were, and a penny a week pocket money. So all things considered, I reasoned we were in a better position than we had been and there was a stability to our lives once more.

But I worried about Dad. I wrote to him to let him know where we were but we didn't have a reply. Then one Saturday morning shortly after, Matron Calcut called me to her office. I couldn't think what I might have done to displease her and asked Daisy Viola if she knew what I was supposed to have done..

'You'll find out when you get there, won't you?' she said.

I knocked on the door and entered.

'I've had a telephone call to say your father has died,' she said coldly, and without a trace of sympathy.

'Yes Matron,' I said. 'When did he die?'

'Yesterday. You've only got us now,' she said, fixing me with her steely gaze, then added, 'And just remember, this is *not* your home, you are only lodgers here.'

With that sad, though not entirely unexpected piece of news, I went back to scrubbing the kitchen floor, where my tears could fall unnoticed. I cried not only because my father had died, but for the cold, harsh hearted way in which I'd been given the news. I also found it hard to understand why she told me not to tell Muriel.

It didn't take me long to grasp the significance of her statement: *You've only got us now.* It was curious how incurious we children were about each others backgrounds and it never occurred to any of us to ask: 'Why are you here?' But there were some children who had occasional visits from some adult relation or other, and the ones who had no visitors were the ones mostly singled out for chastisement.

I often wondered why someone with such a sadistic nature as Matron Calcutt chose to work with children, as she appeared to have no love for them. It occurred to me many years later that she assumed by the very necessity of our being where we were, that we were all flawed characters in need of constant correction. We were allocated daily and weekly tasks to perform about the house and this was only to be expected and no real hardship at all. But it was one thing working at my speed and to my satisfaction and to be praised for it, and something else when everything had to be done with all speed and to the entire satisfaction of someone ever ready to criticise and punish.

Muriel's job was to dust the chapel each day before morning prayers and once a week to polish the brass candlesticks, but she couldn't always finish the latter task before the bell was sounded for breakfast. She was smacked if she lined up for breakfast before she'd finished polishing the candlesticks, and smacked if she finished polishing the candlesticks but failed to get into line on time for breakfast; so I would rush through my job of polishing the shoes in the boot room and then sneak off to help her.

Daisy Viola Rose was the oldest girl in the Home and I think she'd been there the longest and I soon realised she was someone to be feared. She was tall and imposing, her best feature being her thick, brown hair, which, together with her permanently rosy cheeks served to relieve the otherwise plainness of her features.

I felt it was in mine and Muriel's best interests if I could keep on the right side of her and I tried to put the biblical exhortation of St. Matthew into practice whenever I thought about it (which wasn't often) to: "Love your enemies, do good to them that hate you.'

Chapter 10

Portrait of a Thief

I think I must have been about twelve at the time when I entertained the dormitory after lights out by regaling them with one of Angela Brazil's stories about a girls boarding school and their midnight feasts, which gave Daisy Viola the notion that we should have one.

I was pleased to have made such an obvious impression on her with my story telling, but how could we have a feast without any food. As usual, Daisy Viola had the answer – we would have to steal some and as no one volunteered, she decreed that I would have to do it.

Risking punishment for talking after lights out was one thing, but stealing was quite another and I wasn't sure of which I was most afraid, Daisy Viola's derision or the possible consequences of being caught. She told me the food was kept locked in the pantry and the key was to be found hanging on a hook in the kitchen to the left of the dresser.

Unable to think quickly of a good reason why I should not go on my thieving mission, and in a way, I suppose, wishing to ingratiate myself with Daisy Viola, I stealthily made my way down the back stairs and hoped all the staff had gone to bed. I groped my way into the large kitchen and located the keys, but they were out of my reach. I considered trying to jump up and knock them off the hook, then decided against it, for even if I managed to knock them off, how was I to put them back? I found a stool, climbed onto it and reached for the keys, but in my state of fear and excitement, I fell off the edge of the stool which sent me crashing to the ground. I lay there stunned and terrified that one of the staff might have heard the bang, but no one came, so I picked myself up and made my way along the passage until I got to the pantry. With trembling fingers, I fumbled the key into the lock and opened the door.

It was dark and I could barely discern the labels on the tins which stood on a shelf to my right. Too terrified to be selective, I grabbed the first tin that came to hand, then crept back to the kitchen to grab a spoon and a tin opener and put the keys back, being careful not to fall off the stool again.

I got back to the dormitory with my loot feeling a sense of triumph and achievement, but Daisy Viola was not impressed. What I thought might be a tin of baked beans turned out to be a tin of salmon (for staff consumption only). But since we'd got it, we thought we'd eat it anyway, and the tin was duly opened by Daisy Viola. She took the first couple of spoonfuls then handed it on to the person in the next bed. There was no giggling or excitement. The tin was solemnly passed from bed to bed for each to have a meagre share of the contents. By the time it got to me, all that was left was a horrible lump of black skin and some juice. I'd lost my appetite anyway, so I put the spoon in, pretended to eat, then passed the tin on to the girl in the next bed, who ravenously ate the skin, then tilted the tin and drank the juice. Then there was the matter of disposing of the tin and Daisy Viola said that as I was the one who'd stolen it, I should be the one to get rid of it. So down the stairs I went again and put it in the kitchen waste bin.

The so called midnight feast turned out not to be at all like the one described in the Angela Brazil story and no fun at all. When I got back to the dormitory, all was peace and innocence. No one spoke or praised me for being the little heroine I truly believed myself to be and I felt very disappointed and deflated. I got into bed and offered up a fervent 'thank you' to the Almighty for not letting me get caught, then drifted off into a conscience-smitten sleep.

The following morning at breakfast, Matron Calcut rose from her chair looking like the wrath of God and rang her bell loudly for attention. She then announced that there was some very serious business to be dealt with. My heart did a somersault and landed in my mouth, rendering me unable to swallow the porridge I'd just spooned in.

I watched in horror as she raised the empty salmon tin on high, as if it was a sporting trophy, and demanded to know who was responsible for stealing it.

Silence.

'If the person responsible does not own up at once, everyone will be punished,' she threatened.

I glanced under my eyelids at Daisy Viola, who was glaring at me accusingly, blushed to the roots of my hair, made a valiant effort to swallow my lodged porridge, then put my hand up and said, 'Please Matron, it was me.'

A look of cynical satisfaction spread over her hard, righteous features as she ordered me to stand in the middle of the dining room.

'Take a good look,' she commanded. 'Now you can all see what a thief looks like and what happens to thieves. She then hoisted my gym slip in front of everyone and gave me six lashes of the cane on my bare buttocks, after which, she ordered one of the staff to remove my bowl of porridge, as I couldn't possibly be hungry after eating a tin of salmon.

The hurt and humiliation of the beating was as nothing to the mental anguish and shame I felt at being labelled a thief, and more to the point, actually *looking* like one! For a thief indeed I was. For the rest of that day, instead of attending to my school lessons, I thought back to my younger days when I had indulged in a bit of thievery. It was when we had a shop and I snuck in and pinched a handful of boiled sweets from one of the jars, rammed them into my mouth and crunched them up as fast as I could. I then got raging toothache, so although I wasn't actually found out, God obviously knew and gave me the pain as a punishment.

There was also the time I pinched an apple and orange from the greengrocer's horse drawn cart to put in Muriel's Christmas stocking and the bits of coal I took from the slag heap to help keep the fire going; and another time, when Granny was looking after us. She didn't give us our penny a week pocket money, so after a few weeks I asked her for it and she said she couldn't give it to us because she hadn't any money to spare. She told me to fetch her purse to prove it. I found her purse, opened it and saw some money, so I removed a shilling before handing it to her. She didn't find out and I bought a bar of chocolate and a bag of banana split toffees which I shared with Muriel, putting her on pain of death if she 'told'.

She didn't tell, but my theft did not escape the all seeing eye of the Almighty, and my punishment was a further bout of raging toothache. The two offending teeth were eventually removed and I still have the gaps as a permanent reminder of my wicked ways. There were probably other childish incidents of minor larceny which I can't recall, but collectively, the instances I could remember were obviously enough to make me look like a thief. So for a time, I kept looking in the mirror to see what I could do to change my thief betraying features. I made many and varied facial contortions, sometimes downing my lips or trying to make them curl upwards at the sides; other times frowning, and at others lifting my face and my eyebrows, leaning my head back and pretending to be a film star. But nothing worked and in no time at all, my features would revert to their normal shape and there was nothing to be done. I even promised God that if he would please change my features, so that I didn't look like a thief anymore, I would never, *ever*, do anything to displease him again. It made not a scrap of difference. Shortly after, I had an idea. I studied the faces of other children, trying to decide whether I could distinguish in them the thieves from the non-thieves, and try as I might, I could not. So that was it then. If I couldn't tell the difference, I didn't suppose other people could.

I looked in the mirror again and smiled. This time, instead of looking at the face of a thief, I saw the happy smile of optimism.

Chapter 11

Girl Guides

The time came when I was old enough to join the Girl Guides and I happily went along with some of the other girls who already belonged. I was put in the Swallow Patrol and Guide Captain Millie Plester decided we would have a competition to see which patrol could tie the most knots in a given time. I was not acquainted with 'knots' and when the patrol leader told me to tie a *reef knot*, I looked at her in dismay and said I didn't know how.

She dramatically smacked her hand to her forehead and loudly exclaimed, 'Oh my God! I've got someone in my patrol who can't even tie a reef knot!'

My shame knew no bounds. It seemed the whole world knew how to tie a reef knot except me. But I soon put matters right, assiduously learned how to tie every knot there was to be tied and eventually got a badge to sew on my sleeve to prove it.

I wasn't very happy with the navy blue Girl Guide hat I'd been given to wear. It had small indents all over the crown and looked as if it had been rained on very heavily then allowed to dry, dimpled from the raindrops. I mentioned this to Daisy Viola who said she could fix it. So the next time we were we were getting ready to go to Guides, she rammed the hat down on my head as far as it would go, then tried ironing my head with a hot *flat iron*. Not wishing to displease her, or seem ungrateful, I squirmed and bore the pain as long as I could, then screamed out for her to stop. The hat was removed together with some of my scorched hair; I had sore patches on my head and the dimpled hat remained dimpled..

Once a month the Boy Scouts and Girl Guides attended Church Parade and I loved it. My big disappointment however was that I never got to carry the banner, something I longed to do, but was never asked. I put it down to the fact that I probably didn't look smart enough in my dimpled hat..

It was at least fifty years later when I bumped into Miss Plester out shopping. She must have been in her eighties at the time, but still had the ever ready, innocent smile of an eager child. We talked of old times and I laughingly told her how disappointed I was that I had never had the privilege of proudly carrying the 10th Leamington Girl Guide Banner on the monthly church parades.

She looked quite stricken, then said, 'But you should have asked.'

I don't think she realised that it just wouldn't have been the same if I'd had to *ask* for the honour.

Miss Plester, as well as being a guide captain, was a junior school teacher, a dedicated church goer, kind and generous and one of the loveliest people I knew. She treated us 'Home Girls' as equals and never patronised us. So I was really sorry when we once let her down very badly.

It was December and about six of us set off from St. Anne's to go to Guides, but on the way, Daisy Viola Rose, who was unofficially in charge of us, suggested that, rather than going to Guides, we went carol singing instead.

We didn't need any persuading and knocked on the doors of the big houses in the immediate vicinity, where we gave very passable renditions of carols from our considerable repertoire. Seeing our uniforms and doubtless impressed with our singing, most people generously rewarded us for our efforts. At one house, after we'd sung a couple of carols, the door opened and we were invited inside by a smiling, elegant, middle-aged lady. We were ushered into the most gracious living room I had ever seen, with draped gold velvet curtains, luscious sofas covered in green cut brocade, and strewn with pale, plump cushions. A grand piano stood in a corner of the room and the lady made her way to the stool and asked us what carols we would like her to play. We stayed for about ten minutes or more singing round the piano and were afterwards rewarded with mince pies and some money. It was a truly magical experience and one which I will never forget. When we left the house to happy smiles, grateful thanks and cheerful goodbyes, we judged that Guides would be over about now. So after Daisy Viola, who had charge of the money, had shared it out, we made our way back to St. Anne's feeling full of the joys of the season. On the way back to St. Anne's, I even planned in my head what I was going to do with my ill-gotten gains, which included buying a little something for Muriel for Christmas and perhaps an exercise book for myself.

We arrived back at St. Anne's, our stomachs replete with mince pies, cheerfully chattering and congratulating ourselves on what a wonderful time we'd had and what a good idea it had been. I even, briefly, felt a little more kindly towards Daisy Viola.

Our elation didn't last long. We were met on our return by a furious Matron Calcutt who demanded to know where we'd been.

'To Guides, Matron, where we always go on a Friday evening.'

'Liars!' she spat.

'We have – honest Matron,' said one of the bolder members of the party.

I wasn't sure who it was that answered, but as it was my unhappy lot to be standing nearest to Matron, I got a sharp whack across the face as she demanded. 'Now tell the truth! I've had Miss Plester on the telephone wondering where you'd got to.'

The game was up. Any money we owned up to having was promptly confiscated, never to be seen again; we were sent to bed without our nightly cup of cocoa and told we would be dealt with in the morning.

The following morning, a Saturday, our crime was deemed to be so serious that the Vicar – The Reverend Canon Daniels – was sent for and we were duly arraigned before him.

I think he was a kindly man, who looked as if he'd rather be anywhere than where he was, but he had a duty to do. So he stood before us, in all his pink, fat flabbiness and demanded of each of us what we had to say for ourselves. Daisy Viola was the first to be questioned and I couldn't believe it when she said that she'd tried to dissuade us from doing what we did, but when we took no notice she thought she'd better stay with us to make sure we came to no harm.

'Very good. Very good.' he muttered into his double chin.

When it got to my turn to give an account of myself, I was so overwhelmed with guilt over the enormity of our crime, that when I opened my mouth to speak no sound came out.

'Speak up – speak up child,' he said, but still no sound came.

Then Sheila Burden, who was standing next to me and whom I hated, cleared her throat very loudly on my behalf. I found my voice, and, not wishing the Vicar to think badly of me, I squeaked, 'I'm very sorry I went carol singing instead of to Guides Canon Daniels, and promise never to sing carols again.'

'Good. Very good.' he mumbled once more and passed on to the next mortal sinner.

It would be difficult to say we were severely chastised by the Vicar, and his aspect was anything but intimidating, but it was the fact of having been brought before him that filled me with genuine remorse. Matron Calcut awarded us all three black marks in the *punishment book* (all, that is, except Daisy Viola) and deprived us of all privileges for a week, which didn't seem too bad as I wasn't aware that we had any privileges to be deprived of anyway, except our penny a week pocket money.

I felt sorry for Miss Plester, for I'm sure she would have been mortified had she known at the time what a furore she caused in reporting our absence, but I don't suppose she could have imagined that we'd have done anything as evil as going carol singing instead of Girl Guiding.

But there was an unexpected and happy outcome to this episode. Unbeknown to us, it appeared that the lady who'd invited us into her home to sing round the piano happened to be on the committee of St. Anne's Home, and she contacted Matron Calcutt to ask if we could go and sing carols for her again. Our week of privilege deprivation was over and I don't think Matron would want to get on the wrong side of a worthy committee lady anyway, so we were allowed to go.

We learned her name was Mrs. Starkey, and they had some of their relations over for Christmas. She played the piano again, we sang with great gusto, sometimes in unison and sometimes in harmony and were clapped and appreciated and rewarded with all manner of lovely party food. It was one of the very few Red Letter days I ever spent whilst at the 'The Annie's' especially as Daisy Viola Rose hadn't come with us to boss us about and try and grab all the attention. Perhaps I didn't give Matron enough credit for her cunning astuteness, for she called her back just as were leaving and said, 'I don't think you want to go with them Daisy do you, since you weren't in agreement the last time they went carol singing?'
So justice was done after all.

Chapter 12

The Garden Party

The following Summer there was a Garden Party at the Vicarage. For our contribution, we Girl Guides had been practising dancing round the Maypole, holding a strip of coloured ribbon in each hand and weaving in and out of each other to form a sort of tent out of the ribbons. A piano had been dragged out onto the beautifully manicured and spacious lawn and Miss Plester played it whilst we pranced around to the song: *Come lasses and lads get leave of your dads and away to the May Fair go.* All was going well until one of the girls let go of one of her ribbons and it became entangled. So when we danced in the opposite direction to unwind, try as we might, we could not get beyond the entangled ribbon. Round and round we went and when it came to the end of her music, Miss Plester glanced across at us, saw we were not yet unwound, and with a puzzled frown, began thumping away at the piano again, the while we dutifully skipped about and got into further entanglement. I, and I'm sure all the others, were now in a state of utter exhaustion, but while the piano kept playing, we kept moving, and still the recalcitrant ribbon would not disentangle.

. Finally, before we all collapsed with fatigue, who should come to the rescue but Daisy Viola Rose! She told us to stop, called out to Miss Plester to stop playing, then manhandled the tall pole down, pulled free the offending ribbon, acknowledged the applause from the crowd, then said we should finish the dance, which we did without further trouble. It was one of the very rare occasions when she had my admiration and I realised that bullies did sometimes have their uses.

Chapter 13

Life in the Laundry

When I was about thirteen my Saturday morning job was to work in the laundry alongside some of the other girls with one of the staff in charge. No mechanised washing machines in those days, everything was done by hand in a huge tub with the aid of a wooden plunger known as a *dolly stick*. On the first morning, my job was to drag the sheets out of the rinsing tub and feed them into the huge mangle whilst someone else turned the handle. This was all very well, but it was difficult heaving the sheets out of the tub, and being small for my age, even more difficult trying to feed them into the mangle, having to stand on tip toes to reach the rollers. I finally managed to get the first sheet up to the roller but the winder of the handle did it so quickly that the fingers of my left hand got wound in too. They poured with blood, the sheet had to be re-washed and I was sent to Matron by the staff member to get my fingers bandaged. Matron went to the first aid box, and without a murmur of sympathy carefully bound up my fingers, then gave me a good hiding. 'That will teach you to be more careful in future,' she spat. She then added that through sheer carelessness I had rendered myself unfit for work.

I liked the sound of that: *Rendered myself unfit for work,* and for a few moments had visions of myself spending the rest of the day reading and nursing my poorly fingers. My thoughts were quickly dispelled when she changed her mind and said, 'You can do the ironing instead, you don't need two hands for that.'

'Yes Matron.' I said dutifully, taking care to hide my disappointment.

Chapter 14

Puberty and Confirmation

The time came, when, in company with some of the other girls of similar age, I was required to attend weekly instruction classes in the Catechism prior to Confirmation. We were informed on various aspects of the church teaching and drilled on questions and answers, most of which I've forgotten, or now consider irrelevant to my way of life, but I took it all very seriously at the time.

One of the things I remember most clearly about these classes and all the enforced religiosity however, had nothing to do with what we were being taught in this small study in the vicarage. It was when someone's stomach gave an almighty thunderous rumble. I was in direct eye-line to the vicar and he raised his eyes and stared at me, long and accusingly. I squirmed and blushed guiltily and never did find out whose offending stomach it was, but the shame of it possibly being thought to be mine lived with me for some time.

The day of Confirmation arrived and unhappily, it coincided with the day of my first period. I had a vague idea about periods from some of the other girls, but in my ignorance, thought I might be spared this monthly ordeal. I pondered how best to reveal my predicament without too much embarrassment and finally knocked on Matron's door and said, 'Please Matron, I've stained my combinations.'

Without bothering to look up from her desk she said, 'See Miss Clifford.'

I saw Miss Clifford and said the same to her as I'd said to Matron, whereupon, with scarcely a word, Miss Clifford went to a cupboard and handed me six squares of terry towelling with sewn on loops and a piece of elastic. She then found me some knickers and I understood that this was the important time when we made the transition from combinations to proper knickers, and marked our initiation into early adulthood.

I had a bath and hitched myself up to a folded terry towel before donning the white dress in which I was to be confirmed. It was much too big and when I asked if there was a smaller one I was told not to be so vain – I was being *confirmed* not attending a fashion parade.

We assembled in the hall before leaving for the Parish Church and for no reason that I could fathom, were variously subjected to a tirade of verbal abuse (no swear words mind) from Matron. I don't remember all the words of upbraiding, but I do recall being told, accompanied by a stinging whack across the face, that I was a hypocrite. I thought this was a bit much since I had no choice about being confirmed anyway.

All Saints Parish Church, where the Bishop of Coventry was to confirm us, was about a mile walk from St. Anne's, and as we walked, my inner thighs began to chafe and I was worried that the blood might seep through onto the back of the dress. When we reached the church I didn't feel in the least holy or have any sense of occasion, and the only prayer I prayed, and that more fervently, I'm sure, than any other prayer offered that evening by whomsoever else was: 'Please, *please,* God, don't let it show through.' To try to prevent this, I sat, uncomfortably throughout the Service, either on one buttock or the other, the only relief being when we were required to kneel down.

At last, what should have been an uplifting experience but wasn't, was over. On the way back to St. Anne's a sly glance behind revealed all was well and despite all that had gone before, I now felt light-hearted, happy even - happiness being an unstained, pristine white dress.

The following Sunday, we new communicants were invited to breakfast at the vicarage after the Service. I had never seen such a magnificent feast. There were hot, crusty bread rolls, real butter, thick slices of cold ham, hard boiled eggs and a variety of cheeses, with toast and marmalade and coffee, all spread out on a huge dining table covered with a white damask tablecloth. It was the very best meal I had ever had. And to top it all, George, the vicar's son and my favourite choir boy - winked at me across the table.

A month later we were required to attend our next Communion Service at eight o'clock in the morning and were duly marched off in charge of Miss Acheson, one of the less ferocious members of staff. As was the custom in those days, no food or drink must pass our lips before the Service, or we would be deemed to be in a state of un-holiness, and therefore unfit to partake of the Holy Sacrament.

During the service I began to feel weak and a strange sensation flooded my being. The Vicar's voice seemed to alternate between booming loudly and fading, and his figure seemed to loom large then fade away into the distance. The next thing I knew, I felt something pressing hard on the back of my head holding me down, the while I tried to focus on a red and gold pattern that kept swimming before my unfocussed eyes. Bewildered, I thought I must be in a dream and yelled out, 'Where am I?'

'Shut up you little ass! You're in church,' came a hissed reply.

'Where?' I yelled again.

' Church! Now get up and stop making a fool of yourself,' came the next cross whispered command, from whom I now realised was the disciplinarian Miss Acheson.

The pressure was released from the back of my head, and I was helped from the floor back into the pew. I soon realised the puzzling red and gold that had been swimming before my eyes was the pattern worked on the hassock into which my face had been pressed.

When we got back to St. Anne's Miss Acheson reported the incident to Matron and I was sent straight up to the sick room without any breakfast, on the grounds that if I was ill I couldn't possibly be hungry. And there I stayed for hours, starving, bored, fed-up and feeling very hardly done-to. No member of staff came to see if I was all right, or even bring me a drink, never mind some food, and I felt this was a subtle form of punishment rather than confinement to bed for the sake of my health. I think I might have been dozing, when I was alerted by a slight sound. I eagerly turned my head and watched as the door cautiously opened and in crept Muriel bearing a peeled, raw potato, which she held out to me.

' Thanks Mu,' I said, as I ravenously bit into the potato, 'I'm starving. Don't stay in case you get caught.'

She crept away and I worried for a while in case she was found out for pinching. Eventually I heard the bell ring for tea, so I got dressed and took my place in the queue to enter the dining room, hoping I wouldn't be noticed.

'What are you doing out of bed?' demanded Matron.

'Please Matron I got up for tea.'

'Get back to bed at once,' she said, or you won't be fit for school in the morning.

Miserable with hunger and a sense of injustice, I made my way back to the isolation of the sick room and there I remained until I got up on the Monday morning, had my breakfast and went to school as usual, without anyone mentioning a word about the day before.

Chapter 15

On Leaving School.

The time was rapidly approaching when I would have my fourteenth birthday and have to leave school – not a prospect that I looked forward to. It wasn't that I enjoyed school all that much, but I was fearful of what was to come. It was a very elementary school and the education was sketchy almost to the point of being non-existent and we were never given any homework. There was no encouragement from the staff of St. Anne's to do well either, for we were all destined to become domestic servants, and to aspire to anything else was out of the question. In other words, know your place, recognise your limitations and stay within them.

Looking back, although a naturally friendly child, I don't recall making a special friend of anyone either at school or at the Home. And the only teacher I could relate to was Mrs. Dilnot – the gym mistress. I was good at sport, gymnastics and athletics and she took me under her wing and I would do anything to please her. At the inter-school sports I invariably won the sprint races and formed a leg of the 4 X 100 relay races which we often won. And it was all worth it to have a smile and a word of congratulations from Mrs. Dilnot, who also frequently rewarded me with an ice-cream if there was a "Stop-me-and-Buy-One" bicycle in the vicinity. Dear Mrs. Dilnot - who would I look to when there was no one else in my life who seemed to care and who I wanted to please more than she.

I had my fourteenth birthday in November 1937 and left school that Christmas without a qualification to my name, there being no expectation or opportunity for anything other than a basic, elementary knowledge of the three 'R's'. But apart from leaving school, there was another life changing experience for me at St. Anne's. The hard-hearted dragon Matron Calcutt left, and it was rumoured she'd gone to take charge of a so-called 'Naughty Girls Home' in London, where she would, no doubt, have even more opportunity to vent her cruel vengeance on the poor unfortunates committed to her care.

I actually cried when she left, and for the life of me couldn't think why, unless it was that, in spite of her harshness and cruelty, she was a constant in my life, and *who* would we get in her place. At least she was the devil we knew.

Matron Powell came striding into our lives the day after Miss Calcutt left and looked everything Miss Calcutt was not. She was tall and angular, with fine fair hair that seemed to defy all efforts to keep it neatly in place. Her complexion was also fair and sparsely sprinkled with faded freckles. She had blue eyes and wore ordinary clothes as opposed to the severe, intimidating grey uniform of Miss Calcutt. In no time at all, she set about making changes for the better. Even so, I was wary of her at the start, kept a low profile and hoped I wouldn't be noticed as I went about my daily tasks in the house.

On leaving school, our lot was to work full time unpaid in the Home for twelve months, as this was considered a sort of training period prior to being let loose on the big wide world when we were fifteen to work as a domestic servant. One day when I was slaving away in the scullery doing a mountain of washing up, I heard Matron Powell call out, 'Where are you Lynn and what are you doing?'

I automatically assumed I must be in trouble for something or other and timidly squeaked, 'I'm in the scullery Matron, washing up,' and instead of revealing myself, I stayed where I was to prove it.

She popped her head round the scullery door, grabbed a tea towel and said, 'Well let's hurry up and finish and we'll go to the park for a game of tennis.'

I could not believe my eyes or my ears and nearly fell dead on the spot with relief and surprise. Here was the Matron, drying up the dishes with me, speaking to me in a kindly manner and suggesting we go to the park to play tennis. I curbed my desire to throw my arms around her neck in gratitude and said, with what I hoped was a casual air, 'I'd really like to do that Matron, but I've never played tennis before.'

'Well there's always a first time,' she said.

When the washing up was finished she produced two tennis racquets, a net of balls and off we went to the Victoria Park. She walked along briskly and it would be true to say that I floated on air beside her, scarcely able to believe that this was actually happening to me. If there was any conversation between us, I don't remember it. It was enough that I was going to play tennis with her – no matter how badly – and I thought I would love her forever and ever. I quickly learned to play a pretty decent game of tennis but more than this, I began to realise that I had someone to whom I could relate and who gave me some significance as a person, although, at the time it was only something I felt, without the ability to rationalise. She asked me questions about my family, not in an official capacity but in a conversational way, and when I told her how I worried about Muriel and what an ordeal it was for her to eat the porridge every morning, she didn't say anything, but the next morning at breakfast she announced that anyone who didn't like porridge could have a slice of toast and marmalade instead.

Chapter 16

My First Job.

In September 1939 two things happened, the most important of which was that World War 2 was declared. But more pertinent to me was, that at the age of fifteen and three quarters, it was months past the time when, as was normal practice, I should have been placed in domestic service and I began to think, wrongly as it happened, that there might be something better lined up for me. What that might be was past my imagining, but I lived in hope. In the meantime I performed all the menial domestic work set me with vigour and to the very best of my ability. It was the only way I knew of expressing my undying love for Matey Powell (as all we children now dubbed her) for I wanted to impress and please her in every way I could.

But the time came when I had to leave St. Anne's and was found a job as a domestic servant to a childless, middle-aged, lower middle-class couple living in Leamington. He was a Coal Board Official and she, a lady of leisure and highly respected member of St. Anne's Home committee. It was a disappointment but I knew I had to accept my lot and get on with it and above all, be a credit to Matey and St. Anne's.

I had to do everything in the house – cleaning, cooking, serve meals, attend to the fires, polish the silver; you name it – I did it. The first day I was so nervous about serving them the lunch I'd cooked that I dropped the gravy boat and it broke. I was thoroughly chastised for my carelessness, which made me blush with shame and embarrassment, although I took heart in that there was no gravy in it at the time.

The terms of my employment were that I would live-in, be paid ten shillings (50p) a week, and have a half-day off on a Saturday. I looked forward to my very first week's pay on the Friday and thought I would ask Matey for permission to take

Muriel out on my half day on the Saturday. Friday came and although I waited eagerly all day there was no sign of my being paid. So I thought perhaps I had misunderstood and I would be paid on the Saturday instead. Saturday came. I did my morning jobs, cooked their lunch, washed up afterwards and waited to be paid before taking my 'half-day.' Still no wages, so after waiting a little while longer, I timorously inquired, 'Please Mrs. Woods, may I start my half-day now and will you be paying me before I go?'

'Oh no,' she replied indignantly. 'It's standard practice. You have to work a week in hand before you're paid and your work has to be entirely satisfactory.'

Instead of going out, I went up to my bedroom, threw myself on the bed and cried with disappointment.

I worked harder than ever during the ensuing week, trying to prove I was worthy of the job, and when Friday came, I once more waited eagerly to receive my wages, but still they weren't forthcoming. So again, I waited until the Saturday before broaching the subject again.

This time she said, 'Surely you don't expect any wages do you? You broke my best gravy boat and it will cost more than your wages to replace it.'

So I'd worked all week to replace a broken gravy boat!

I went up to my tiny bedroom and once more threw myself on the bed and cried. The height of my immediate ambition had been to buy Muriel a *Knickerbocker Glory* at the local milk bar, something I promised her I would do with my first wages and which, at the time, seemed to me to be the epitome of luxury and sophistication.

I dried my eyes, stopped moping and went out for a walk, but I didn't go to see Muriel for I didn't want her to see how unhappy I was, or to see how disappointed she would be that I couldn't take her to the milk bar. And I certainly didn't want to see Matey for I wanted her to think I was doing well. After my long, lonely walk I felt a little better about things and made my way back to the house of misery.

The following day, when I was busying myself in the kitchen making the best job I could of cooking the Sunday lunch, Mrs. Woods appeared in the doorway with something red hanging over her arm. I thought she'd come to carp and criticise that I was taking too much peel off the potatoes or something, but instead, her tone was soft and almost kindly.

'I'd like you to have this dress,' she said. It's practically new, but it no longer fits me and I think it would look very nice on you.'

I hadn't much in the way of clothes admittedly, but when I looked at the dress my heart sank. It was a red, thick wool knitted dress with long sleeves and a turn down collar, and whilst doubtless it would probably have looked fine on a lady of advancing years, I was sure it wouldn't look at all right on me. She held it against me and the skirt reached down to within a few inches of the floor, but she told me how well the colour suited me, and, grateful for being spoken to in an unusually kindly manner, I accepted it with as much courtesy as I could force myself to display, then went back to concentrating on the cooking.

Pay day came round again and I was past being disappointed when she said, 'You surely don't expect to be paid as well as my giving you that lovely dress do you? It would take several weeks wages for you to buy a dress of that quality.'

I went to my room, threw the hateful dress on the floor and stamped all over it, knowing I would never wear it.

By now, I was desperate for some money. I'd started my period, had not been given any terry-towelling squares when I left St. Anne's and needed money to buy some sanitary towels. I was too embarrassed to say so, especially in front of her husband, so thought I would try and manage by stuffing toilet roll strategically inside my knickers, then washing them every night. I only had two pairs, so I would wash one pair and try drying them quickly on the kitchen range ready for the next day, while wearing the other pair in bed. But I left them on the range too long and they got scorched black. So I was then left with one pair of knickers and really didn't know how I was going to manage. Mrs. Woods had gone to bed and I sat in the kitchen, staring unbelievingly at my burnt knickers and sobbing softly when Mr. Woods appeared to see why the kitchen light was still on. He asked me why I was still up and why was I crying and wasn't I happy with them. I was anything but, though I didn't think it in my best interests to say so, and I couldn't possibly explain the reason for my tears, so I said I was missing my sister, not having seen her for three weeks.

He put his arms around me and drew me to him and for a brief moment I fell against his ample chest and let him hug me. But then he alarmed me by trying to kiss me. I didn't want to seem ungrateful for his sympathy, but this, I felt, was going beyond sympathy so I wriggled from his grasp and went up to my room. I was scared and thought he might come into the bedroom, so I quickly packed what few belongings I had (less the red dress) and when I heard him go into the bathroom I flew down the stairs and out into the night.

I reached the safety of the pavement and ran until I was out of breath, then stopped and wondered where I was running to. Certainly not St. Anne's. I felt too embarrassed to tell Matey Powell what had happened. Besides, Mrs. Woods was a local magistrate and if I did tell, who would be believed? I also thought I might be sent to a Naughty Girls Home for *further training*, which I knew had happened to one of the other girls when she left her job without permission, and I didn't want the disgrace of that.

I briefly considered going back to the place I'd just run from but knew there was no way of gaining access without ringing the doorbell, so I wandered off to the local park, found a bench in a far corner and lay down on it, using my small travel bag as a pillow and my coat as a covering. Now I had the time to indulge in self-pity and fear. Fear for the night and whether I would survive it; fear that I might be discovered and fear for the enormity of what I had done and the possible consequences. Overcome with weariness, I must have slept for I had a lovely dream. I was back in our house in Wales with both my parents and they were telling me they hadn't died - it was all a big mistake by the hospital.

The long night ended. I was cold, uncomfortable, hungry and scared, and had no idea what I should do or what was to become of me as I walked aimlessly through the park.

A slight mist gave way to the morning sun, which reflected on the still, deep waters of the River Leam. I watched the swans gliding effortlessly over the water, and I looked at the weeping willows skirting the banks of the river, their slender drooping branches dancing over the small ripples. As I stood there, a sense of beckoning calm washed over me. I edged nearer to the bank and stood, watching the bewitching water... It would be so easy... Then I thought of my sister – how could I leave her alone in the world.

My mind was made up and I slowly made my way to St. Anne's to face whatever fate had in store for me. I felt ashamed of my bedraggled appearance and was so worried that I had proved less than had been expected of me. I also worried that if I did get sent to a Naughty Girls Home it might even be the one where Miss Calcutt was in charge.

When I reached St. Anne's I didn't even have to ring the door bell, for Matey Powell was already standing at the top of the steps. When she saw me coming she ran down the steps and flung her arms about me, saying, 'Here you are. Where have you been? I've been so worried about you.'

I told her about not being paid, but left out the bit about Mr. Woods trying to kiss me, for I thought I might be held to blame, so I said only that he'd shouted at me for staying up late and wasting the electricity. I must have told her about other reasons for my unhappiness though, for she said:

'You poor thing, I should never have sent you there.'

'Why did you?' I asked.

'Because they were childless and I thought they might eventually want to adopt you.'

I said nothing, but thought, that if this had been the plan, what a lucky escape I'd had.

Chapter 17

Job Number Two

I stayed at St. Anne's for the next few days whilst they cast around for another job for me, and was very grateful that I wasn't going to be sent to a Naughty Girls Home, but I also dreaded being sent to a private house to work again. As luck would have it, there was an advertisement in the local paper for a Ward Orderly at the local hospital, so I begged to be allowed to go for an interview, and to my relief, I was taken on.

There were several other girls at the hospital doing the same job, most of whom came from County Durham. The wage was the standard domestic rate of ten shillings a week, food and accommodation all found and we were housed in a large dormitory attached to the hospital. The girls were a rough and ready lot and spoke with broad Geordie accents, sometimes a bit difficult to understand, but I rubbed along with them okay, kept myself pretty much to myself and was fortunate, after a few weeks, to be told by the hospital Matron that if I wished, I could sleep on my own in the small room which was attached to the end of the dormitory. I was pleased about this as I could have my privacy without being totally isolated. Many of these girls wanted to keep in touch with home but found letter writing a problem, and of course, very few working class people had telephones in those days, so often I would write their letters for them.

One girl in particular was always asking me to write letters home for her and I felt it was getting a bit much, so the next time she asked me I said I was too busy.

'Oh go on,' she said, 'I'll buy you a bar of chocolate if you'll do it.'

So I did it, but I never saw the promised bar of chocolate.'

The next time she asked me to write a letter I said, 'No,' very firmly.

'Oh *please*,' she said.

'No,' I said again. 'I only wrote the last letter because you said you'd give me a bar of chocolate out of your week's sweet ration – but you didn't.'

'Ah well' she said, totally unfazed, 'You know I tell lies don't you.'

I smiled at her cheek and wrote the letter.

Although the work at the hospital was quite arduous, cleaning the wards, toilets, public areas etcetera, I was used to hard work and it would not be true to say I was unhappy in my job, but I still felt I was capable of being something more than a hospital cleaner. So out of my weekly wage of ten shillings less stoppages, I paid 2/6 (25p) a week to attend evening classes to learn clerical skills, including typing, shorthand and business English. At the time, I had no idea how I would put these skills to good use, but I continued to attend this seedy little office and be taught by this equally seedy, middle-aged gentleman, who never passed up an opportunity to lay his grubby, nail-bitten fingers on any available part of one's anatomy. But I persevered and was eventually given a sort of Diploma which proved I'd completed the preliminary course, and proved to myself that I actually had a brain and what was more, the ability to use it, although how and in what capacity at this stage, I had no idea. I also spent a lot of my off-duty time in the public library, mostly reading in the reference room, trying to fill in the gaps of my sketchy education.

In the meantime, Matron Powell left St. Anne's to marry a vicar and went to live in Worcester. We remained friends and kept in touch throughout the whole of her life until she died years later, in her eighties. Ironically, the youngest of her three sons is the gardener at the almshouses where I now live.

I visited St. Anne's about once a week to see Muriel whilst I was working at the hospital and was relieved, for her sake, to find that the new matron appeared to be of a reasonable disposition, and I hoped she wouldn't be too harsh on the children after they'd got used to the lovely Matey Powell.

Chapter 18

A Night to Remember

On the 7th November 1940 I reached my seventeenth birthday and it was Muriel's birthday on the 10th of the month. The war had been on for just over a year but so far, nothing much had happened to affect our lives in Leamington Spa. Of course, food was rationed, we had to carry a gas mask wherever we went; there were no street lights and all windows had to be blacked out. Other than that, so far, life in the town went on pretty much as before.

The lovely Matey Powell had left St. Anne's after getting married and I wasn't all that impressed with what I'd seen of her replacement, although it was no longer of much consequence to me – it was only my sister I was concerned for. I'd managed to save a little money so I asked Miss Brown – the new Matron - if I could take Muriel to the Theatre in Coventry to see the ballet as a special birthday treat. Discipline in Children's Homes was much stricter in those days than it appears to be now, and I was grudgingly granted permission provided I got her back by 10pm at the latest. I did not think this would be a problem and readily agreed.

So come the day, unused as we were to spending a little sisterly time together, we set off on the bus for Coventry full of excitement and joyful anticipation. I'd used up my week's sweet ration coupons to buy us each a penny bar of Nestles chocolate to eat during the performance, but so entranced were we with the ballet dancing and the beautiful, haunting Tchaikovsky music, our chocolate bars were forgotten and remained in our gas mask boxes. Part way through the performance, the eerie, mournful wail of an air raid siren mingled with the enchanting music, then louder, more terrifying noises pervaded the theatre. The curtain came down and a man came on stage to announce that an air raid was in progress and we were advised to leave the theatre.

We stumbled into the street to a terrifying scene of utter chaos. Clusters of incendiary bombs rained down, bursting into bright orange flowers of fire. Brave wardens rushed about trying to douse the flames with buckets of sand or stirrup pumps. The noise was unbearable, what with the terrifying screams of the panicking people, the brutal drone of the planes and the thunderous thwack as bombs hit buildings. In the mayhem and panic we lost our bearings completely. I rushed up to a Warden to ask the way to Pool Meadow bus station.

'No good going there,' he shouted. 'The buses have stopped running.'

'How do I get to the railway station then?' I shouted.

'No good going there either,' he said. 'Best get into a shelter quick.'

At that moment the blast from a bomb took me off my feet and I flew backwards to the ground, banging my head on the pavement kerb, but so scared was I, that I didn't even notice the pain. A young man in RAF uniform picked me up and threw me against the wall of a standing building, placed his hands above my head and shielded me with his body. My knees were knocking uncontrollably and my teeth were chattering with raw fear, but I managed to recover my senses sufficiently to squeak, 'My sister, my sister, I've lost my sister!'

In a brief lull from the bombing, I managed to wriggle free from his protective body and rushed about calling her name. But she was nowhere to be found.

'Don't worry,' said my protector, 'She can't be far away, we'll soon find her.'

'Oh God! Please, *please,* let me find her,' I pleaded, as I fled down a shelter to see if she had somehow found her way in. But there was no sign of her there. When I came out, the airman was nowhere to be seen and I spent goodness knows how much time rushing about in a blur of panic and fear. Someone shouted, 'Follow us love,' and I joined a gaggle of people who were scurrying away from the noisy, fiery hell to I knew not where. I joined them, urged on with an instinct for survival, knowing that any moment could be my last.

We reached open country and I asked a man if they knew where we were. 'On the Kenilworth Road,' he answered. 'Where d'you want to get to?'

When I told him I wanted to get to Leamington, he assured me I was going in the right direction but said I had at least another eight miles to go. I hastened on in the vague hope that Muriel might be somewhere amongst the fleeing people. She wasn't.

Overhead, the German bombers droned on relentlessly, some towards the city to wreak more havoc, others, mission accomplished, flew in the opposite direction. Spurts of ack-ack fire peppered the night sky each time a plane was spotted in the criss-cross of the searchlights, but we never had the satisfaction of seeing a blazing aeroplane drop from the sky.

Gradually, the number of people walking, some pushing bikes heavily laden with blankets etcetera, diminished as they bedded down in fields and under hedges for the night. There was nothing left for me to do but keep walking.

At last, I reached Leamington and made my way to St. Anne's Home, where all was peace and quiet. Not a chink of light to be seen, all windows, as was obligatory, draped in thick black-out curtains. I mounted the stone steps to the front door and raised my hand to pull the door bell – then dropped it again. How could I explain I'd lost Muriel in the Coventry bombing, yet here I was, safe, and, apart from a sore head, comparatively unscathed. I knew instinctively she wasn't there, so I turned away from the door and in an agony of despair, found myself re-tracing my steps in the direction of Coventry.

I had to find Muriel, I thought, or die in the attempt. My instinct for self-preservation had now been replaced with self-loathing, in that I'd fled from the fiery jaws of hell without doing more to try and find her. By now, there weren't many people left walking, but the few I saw, I asked the same question, knowing I would get the same answer.

I was tired and hungry and sank down on a grassy bank to rest. It was then that I remembered the chocolate bar, which I ate, and wondered if Muriel had eaten hers before...before...whatever had befallen her. I closed my eyes and prayed, without expectation of an answer, since I'd hardly been answered in the past. Before I knew it, I must have dozed off and came to when a faceless lady in white shook my shoulder urging me to wake up. I opened my eyes and was disappointed to find there was no one there.

I got to my feet, and to keep my spirits up and in the hope I might influence God in my favour, I started to sing hymns, and strode on to the rhythm of the tune. I remember one of the hymns I sang, thinking it rather appropriate:

> *Be thou my guardian and my guide,*
> *And hear me when I call;*
> *Let not my slippery footsteps slide,*
> *And hold me lest I fall.*

I stopped singing when I thought I heard footsteps other than mine and peered into the darkness. By the light of the veiled moon, I discerned a woman with a very tall man walking beside her. Even if they couldn't help me, I was pleased to have someone to talk to and hastened towards them.

'Excuse me, have you seen a little girl of about ten on your travels?'

Before the lady could answer, I looked at the man and realised that I'd thought him very tall because he had a child on his shoulders, whose head was nodding forward as if in sleep.

He raised his hands above his head, lifted the drowsy burden from his shoulders and set her down on the bank.

'Would this be....?'

I looked at the bedraggled little bundle and cried out, 'Muriel! Muriel! Wake up – it's me.'

My relief and gratitude knew no bounds, and I kept foolishly repeating, 'It's a miracle. It's amazing. Thank you. Thank you. Thank you so much.'

'It's no more than anyone would have done,' they said.

We came to the parting of the ways and when Muriel and I were on our own, I asked her if she'd eaten her chocolate. A childish question, but it seemed important. She hadn't, so I suggested she eat it all up without even giving me a piece – so she did.

Then, after much thought, I said, 'Best not say that I lost you in Coventry eh, or they might not let me take you out again.' She agreed.

We reached St. Anne's and tugged at the doorbell. At this ungodly hour it clanged embarrassingly loudly and eventually brought a cross, torch bearing member of staff to the door.

'You should have been back at 10 o'clock,' she said severely. 'Where have you been until now?'

'I'm ever so sorry we're so late Miss,' I replied. 'There weren't any buses or trains due to the air raid so we had to walk from Coventry.'

'It took you long enough,' she retorted. 'D'you realise what time it is?

Chapter 19

Croquet on the Lawn

On leaving St. Anne's I'd also left the Girl Guides, but was pleased, one day, when I bumped into Miss Winnie Kerruish. She was something in the hierarchy of the Guide movement and occasionally visited our group, probably to inspect us and hand out any badges awarded for various achievements. I got on well with her and she seemed to like me, so I was happy to accept her invitation to have tea with her and her family on my half day. I cycled the eight miles from Leamington to the village of Snitterfield and was surprised when I saw the magnificent house in which they lived with its massive, manicured lawns and beautifully laid out flower beds.

I think Winnie Kerruish was probably in her late twenties, and I found it rather flattering that someone so much older and who lived in such opulence should want to befriend me. With this thought in mind, I hesitantly rang the door bell in case I was at the wrong house, but I realised I was at the right place when a youngish man opened the door and said, 'You must be Lynn. Come on through, we're playing croquet out the back.' I was introduced to the door opener as brother – William – and after a few pleasantries were exchanged, I sat and watched them finish their game, after which, they invited me to play. I'd never played before, but with a lot of friendly encouragement, I soon got the hang of it and really enjoyed the experience.

We were called in for tea and I was then introduced to parents. Her father was a cheerful, florid faced, rotund man, whilst her mother was awesome, stately and dignified. I was ushered into a palatial drawing room where afternoon tea was served and although food was rationed and in short supply, there seemed to be no shortage of delicately cut sandwiches and a Victoria jam sponge cake to follow. I could still scarcely believe this was happening to me. Mrs. Kerruish asked me where I worked and if I was happy in my job, and not wishing to burden her, or embarrass myself by answering in the negative, I politely replied that, 'Yes, I was quite happy for the time being, but I was looking to do something different in the future.'

Tea over, a short lapse in the conversation, and I was beginning to wonder if I should stay a little longer; offer to help with the washing up, or make my excuses and leave.

The dilemma was soon resolved when Mrs. Kerruish offered to show me round the house, which impressed me no end. We finished up in a study where she invited me to sit down. She quizzed me further about my background and my work and I told her that I wouldn't always be doing that sort of job as I'd got some *qualifications* now. She didn't seem impressed with this statement and I was soon to find out why, for her next question was:

'How would you like to come and work here? Our last maid left to go and work in a munitions factory, but I can see you're much too refined for that.'

So this was what it was all about. How could I have been crass enough to imagine that Miss Winnie Kerruish had wanted me for a friend, when all the time she had probably thought I would come in useful as a replacement maid! Or had I done her an injustice.

Winnie and William (whom I learned was studying for the priesthood) saw me to the door, thanked me for coming and hoped I'd enjoyed myself. 'Yes, I have, and thank you very much.' I said, hiding my disappointment.

'We must do this again,' said Winnie, as I mounted my bike. 'Yes, we must,' I called back, knowing I would never see them again.

Chapter 20

A New Life

June 1941. I was seventeen and a half and old enough to join the forces. I applied to join the WAAF and on August 12th 1941 was sent to RAF Training Establishment Innsworth, Gloucester.

After the obligatory medical examination I was passed A1 fit. My height was recorded as five feet one inch and my weight as seven stone six pounds. Then came the form filling before being interviewed to decide what trade category would be deemed most suitable to education, level of intelligence and work experience. When it came to the question Civilian Occupation – I over-looked my real occupation and wrote: *Student*. After all, I reasoned, I had been studying English, Shorthand and Typing, even it was only for two hours a week in a pokey, privately run little establishment in a back street of nowhere.

My deception obviously worked, for after an intelligence test, I was told I would be accepted as a General Clerk. I was pleased for this was the step up I was looking for from my lowly status. I was in a new world. No one knew my background and I didn't feel the need to reveal it. I could now be whatever people thought me to be and not what my background would suggest. And I was even more happy when I got issued with my uniform. Being very slim, it sat well on me and I felt smart, comfortable and on equal terms with all my contemporaries. And it was the first *new* clothing I'd had since I was ten. I enjoyed the drilling and marching and even the discipline, which, although sometimes petty in the extreme, didn't really bother me all that much, for it was something I'd grown accustomed to both at St. Anne's and at the hospital. After our initial basic training, we were required to go on parade every morning after breakfast for more marching and drilling, after which, details of our postings to various parts of the country were barked out, and those of us who hadn't yet got a posting were allocated menial tasks to be performed around the station. This was when I first met Angela. She was older than me, had an air of superiority and a firm belief that she was worthy of doing something much more important than the task we'd been given, which was to clean the ablutions. I would have done them quite happily, but she went back to our billet protesting vehemently, 'I didn't join up to clean lavatories!'

Because I quite liked her and wanted it to be thought that I, too, was used to better things, I stiffened my back, looked into her rebellious blue eyes and agreed: 'Neither did I!'

'Right,' she said. 'It's a lovely day. We'll break out of camp and hitch a lift somewhere.'

We found a hole in the hedge that surrounded the camp, wiggled our way through and were out on the open road, where we hitched a lift and ended up in Oxford. We drifted round the shops and every now and then I turned to look at myself in the shop windows and was pleased with the reflection. I admired the magnificent architecture of the university colleges and could well understand how the poet – Matthew Arnold – was moved to describe Oxford as *The city of dreaming spires.*

It wasn't long, however, before I got tired, hungry and anxious and secretly wished I was safely back on camp cleaning the lavatories. We had a little money between us, which enabled us to buy a pot of tea and a shared scone in one of Oxford's charming tea rooms, then we made our way to the River Cherwell where we sat on the bank and watched the boats drift by and said how lovely everything was.

But I would still rather have been back on camp, performing the task we'd been allocated, no matter how irksome and demeaning it might have seemed to Angela. I'd had enough of *happiness* and suggested if we started hitching straight away, we might arrive back at camp in time for the evening meal. We walked for what seemed like miles, until eventually a lorry picked us up and took us as far as Gloucester, from where we had to walk the last few miles. We entered camp the way we left it – through the hole in the hedge and I was pleased we were back in time for the evening meal for I was ravenous. Happily, it appeared we had not been missed and seemingly, no one in authority had noticed that the ablutions had not been cleaned.

The following morning was the same routine. Polishing of the brass buttons on our uniform, shining of the shoes, stacking of the three so-called *biscuits* which at night formed a mattress, all in perfect alignment with the other beds, all arranged in military rows down either side of the Nissan Huts. This routine was followed by an *Inspection* by the NCO in charge, after which came breakfast, then drilling and marching and orders for the day. Despite all this strictly imposed discipline, I half suspected that a lot of it was to cover up the chaos that simmered beneath the surface and that they were hard-pushed to know what to do with us all. So when we were on morning parade and she and I were allocated the task of cleaning the windows of our Nissan hut, which was something else she felt beneath her dignity, I weakly agreed that we would make for the hole in the hedge again.

This time Angela and I soon got a lift and finally fetched up in Stratford-on-Avon. I'd had the forethought to bring my Post Office Savings Book with me which held the grand sum of ten shillings; so I drew out seven shillings and sixpence, which enabled us to go to a nice café and have tomatoes on toast and a cup of coffee and still have some money left over.

Shortly, two young men in army uniform strolled in and asked if they could join us at our table. We agreed and they told us they were officers in the Czechoslovakian Army stationed at Wellesbourne. I was quite pleased to talk to them as, before joining up, I had already become friendly with a soldier in the Czech Army who was stationed at the same camp and I asked if they knew Stefan Kopervas. To my surprise, they confirmed they did. They stayed with us, took us on a boat on the River Avon and afterwards treated us to tea and cake at a nice riverside café. Before leaving them to hitch back to camp, I wrote down my Service number and address at Innsworth and asked them if they would pass it on to Stefan, as I'd left to join up without saying goodbye.

We got a bus to the outskirts of Stratford then walked for miles without getting a lift. It was nearly dusk, we were tired and I'd developed painful blisters on the back of my heels. We sat down on a grass verge to rest, and Angela, far from being the sophisticated, worldly person I thought her to be, started to cry and in that moment I went right off her. She was still crying when we dragged ourselves to our feet and hobbled on, until at last, a car stopped. The driver was an elderly man who told us he was a farmer, and although he was only going as far as Gloucester, he took pity on us and drove us all the way to Innsworth. We missed the evening meal and went to bed tired, hungry and dispirited and I decided I would not be going on any more stupid escapades, risking the possibility of blighting my life in the WAAF before it had scarcely begun.

The following morning, the blisters on my heels were so painful that I spoke to my immediate superior – Corporal Gunn – to ask permission to report sick. As were many of our so called superiors vested in brief authority, she was officious and unsympathetic and told me that for someone who wanted to report sick I looked remarkably fit. I agreed I was fit but explained I wanted to report sick because I had really painful blisters on my heels from all the marching.

'Right! Number?' she asked..

'451880'

'Name?'

'Trowbridge.'

'Trowbridge! Trowbridge!' she exploded. 'What are you doing here?'

'Waiting to be posted, Corporal.'

'You should not be here; you were posted to Harrogate yesterday. Get your travel warrant from the Admin office at once and get yourself off to Harrogate before they issue a warrant for your arrest for being absent without leave.'

I didn't need telling twice, forgot all about my blisters and reporting sick, and got on the next train to take me to Harrogate. I didn't even look for Angela to say goodbye. On the train journey I had time to reflect on how stupid I had been to have allowed myself to be so easily led astray and made up my mind it would not happen again.

Chapter 21

My First Posting

After the dreary Innsworth Training Camp with its rows and rows of Nissan Huts, massive parade ground, marching, drilling, bullying and barked orders by anyone with the slightest authority, Harrogate, by comparison, was a dream posting. A lovely, gracious town, the RAF had commandeered many of the best hotels to be used as Medical Training Establishments for doctors and nurses already qualified in civilian life, but who were to be indoctrinated in the ways and requirements of the RAF; they were also used as offices and, of course, as billets.

I was lucky enough to be billeted in The Grand Hotel, which was set in spacious grounds, had tennis courts at the back and over-looked the lovely Valley Gardens at the front. There were usually four of us sharing a bedroom, which was quite a luxury after having had to sleep in dormitories for a goodly part of my life up until now. But I grumbled, along with the rest of the girls about any real or imagined inconveniences. It seemed the thing to do, to pretend that one was used to better things, although I never spoke about my background and people could judge me for what I now appeared to be, without any preconceived notions as to how I should be. Oddly, I found wearing a uniform quite liberating and I felt I could now be on equal terms and hold my own with anyone.

I now had the opportunity to put to good use the skills I had learned at night school, and elevate myself from the *domestic servant* category for which I'd been destined. I worked in the Admin Office and was mostly responsible for typing reports and letters, filling in forms, working out routes and train times and issuing railway warrants to personnel who had finished their courses and were then posted to various parts of the country. Bradshaw's Railway Timetable became my Bible, but due to the vagaries of the wartime train services, it is doubtful whether anyone actually reached their far flung destinations at the estimated time of arrival. And given my appalling sense of direction, it's a wonder they reached them at all!

In order to be upgraded, I had to learn about RAF office procedures and familiarise myself with King's Regulations and try to remember the things I was most likely to be questioned on. To this day, over seventy years later, I still remember, word for word, certain relevant sections of the regulations, one in particular, which came under the heading: 'The Object of a File' which read: *The object of a file is to present the complete history of one particular aspect of a subject, under one heading, in a manner that facilitates easy reference and preserves the correspondence therein from mutilation or defacement.* Pompous language for a pompous publication, but it served the purpose at the time and served me well in my subsequent working life, although, with today's modern technology, I suppose it would now be totally irrelevant.

I had my eighteenth birthday in the November whilst I was stationed in Harrogate, but I kept quiet about it as there were no cards to mark the occasion and I didn't want people wondering why. Christmas was a bit more tricky. I had a card from Muriel, which, together with the postage must have cost her a month's pocket money, one from Matey Powell (who was now Mrs. Moseley and had had the first of her three babies) and one from Stefan Kopervas (the Czech soldier with whom I was friendly) and that was it. The girls sharing my room had spread their cards over their lockers so when they asked me why I hadn't put mine up, I shrugged and said I hadn't got round to it yet. Not wishing to be questioned again, I bought some cards and posted them to myself.

It served the purpose and was, in a weird sort of way, quite comforting to have cards from all these relations – even if they were imaginary. It was only on Christmas Eve, when all the girls with whom I shared a billet and the ones I worked with in the office had gone home, that I allowed myself to indulge a feeling of utter aloneness. It was a brilliant, moonlit night and I walked out of the Hotel, over the road and into the Valley Gardens, where I sat on a bench and cried, bitterly. I cried for my mother, and I cried for my father; I cried for Muriel and I cried for myself and shouted at God. I might have carried on ranting, had I not been startled by a stranger appearing out of nowhere, who asked me if I was all right.

'I twisted my ankle,' I lied. 'but I'm all right now, thank you.'

To discourage further conversation, I got up and convincingly limped back to The Grand Hotel and went to bed. It was over. I'd cried the sorrow out of my soul and the next day I was back to my cheerful self and resolved never to cry for them, or myself again.

I really enjoyed my stay in Harrogate. One of the male sergeants was a musician in civilian life, and as we were obliged to go on Church Parade once a month, he formed a church choir from those of us who had an interest in singing. He was obviously well versed in church music and taught some of us to sing descants to some of the hymns, which I really loved doing. He also ran a concert party, which I was pleased to join, and we put on operettas such as Whitehorse Inn, The Desert Song, Careless Rapture and The Merry Widow. I never aspired to be a star performer, but I really enjoyed all the singing and dancing in the chorus and it did a lot for my confidence and self-esteem. However, now and again things would go wrong and I remember one such occasion when we were performing The Desert Song. Three of us were dancing seductively around Red Shadow, whilst one of the protagonists was singing: *If one flower grows alone in your garden, it's fragrant sweetness will soon pass away...* Red Shadow was not interested in polygamy, and was supposed to brush us aside with an imperious gesture from the back of his hand as we beguilingly gyrated around his person. In one performance, I danced just a bit too close to him. His hand made inadvertent contact with my body and sent me flying backwards off the stage, where I landed, in a dishevelled heap, on top of the big bass drum. I don't know who was the more shocked – Red Shadow, the orchestra, the audience or me! Fortunately, I didn't break the drum and the only real injury I suffered was to my pride. But the applause I got when I bravely clambered back onto stage and carried on dancing was almost worth the indignity I'd suffered.

Chapter 22

Second Posting

In the summer of 1942 my happy days at Harrogate came to an end when our unit moved to the delightful seaside town of Sidmouth, in Devon. Again, we had commandeered the best hotels for offices and accommodation and I couldn't believe how lucky I was to have been sent to such desirable places at opposite ends of the country.

Our musical sergeant, whose name I can't recall, did not come with us, so that was the end of my glory days on the stage. But those of us who'd been in the church choir in Harrogate went on to join the church choir in Sidmouth. All went well until the occasion when I was obliged to miss a choir practice because I was on duty.

On the Sunday, I settled in the choir stalls with the rest of the choristers and all went well until it came to the last hymn – *Crown Him With Many Crowns.* This was one of the hymns to which we had learned a descant in Harrogate, so just before it came to the last verse, Agnes, the girl standing next to me looked at me briefly, raised her eyes in question, and mouthed, 'Descant? Thinking it had already been practised, I nodded briefly in agreement. It came to the last verse – Crown Him the Lord of Hosts – and Agnes led me into the descant, I'm sure a good octave too high. The organist faltered, the choir and small congregation stopped singing, and she and I were left screeching the descant alone. I felt myself going red, my bottom lip was quivering up and down, and having started, we couldn't stop until we'd finished. I felt absolutely mortified, and to compound my shame and embarrassment, when we were leaving the church a few members of the congregation said, 'We *did* enjoy your duet.'

Duet indeed! It transpired that it hadn't been rehearsed at the practice at all – it was only Agnes's idea, and we might well have got away with it if we hadn't been screeching so loudly. Anyway, I was so embarrassed that I never went back to the choir and joined the station military band instead, quickly got the hang of playing the side drum and soon became the lead drummer.

About twice a month we would march around the streets of Sidmouth, with the station band playing marching tunes like the RAF March Past, Colonel Bogey, Hearts of Oak and many others that have escaped my memory, with the drum major proudly swinging his mace at the head of affairs. I would *really* have liked to have been the one swinging the mace, but they wouldn't let me as they said I was too small. I think the general idea was to boost the morale of the civilian population and to remind the residents of the idyllic little town that there was a war on and we were there, in force and in uniform, to defend them. Otherwise, apart from food rationing, lack of the summer holiday makers and the rolls of barbed wire strewn across the beach in case of invasion, it would be difficult to imagine all the fighting that was going on in Europe and the bombing of the big cities.

Whether our marching did or did not lift the spirits of the locals, it was difficult to determine, but it certainly did a lot for me. I was just so thrilled to be beating out the rhythms on the drum and I would feel the throb permeating my whole being.

It was strange in a way, that in volunteering to serve in HM Forces, one was prepared to face whatever dangers might befall. But so far, due to my soft postings, I'd had much more fearful times as a civilian, for apart from the bombing in Coventry in 1941, I'd also spent a terrifying night on Snow Hill Station, Birmingham, with bombs raining down and fires raging all around. A number of people had been killed and injured, and we passengers would be called up from the shelters to get on the train, and then sent scuttling back again when another wave of bombs rained down. My train to Leamington was due out early evening but it was the early hours of the morning before I was finally able to board it and be transported to the safety of Leamington.

By contrast, the scariest moment I'd had since joining up, was when I was lying sunbathing with some friends on the grassy slopes of Salcombe Hill. I thought I felt something wet on my neck and put up my hand to investigate. The *something wet* turned out to be a snake, probably an adder or a grass snake, but I was too terrified to find out which. I leapt up from the ground screaming like a demented banshee, 'A snake! A snake! A snake!' while I fled down the hill as if all the flames of hell were licking at my backside.

Chapter 23

First Love

In June 1942 aged eighteen and a half, I finished all my exams which qualified me to become a fully fledged clerk and I was accordingly promoted to Leading Aircraft Woman. It was about this time I first got to know Denise. Aged twenty four, she was five or six years my senior. Sophisticated and worldly, tall, slim, fair-haired with piercingly blue eyes and an enchanting smile, I couldn't imagine why she should have chosen me as her special friend. For I was the exact opposite, still being, at the time, rather naïve, unworldly, and ready to be impressed.

In contrast with her striking appearance I was small, with dark curling hair, brownish eyes and, given the colour of my hair and eyes, I suppose I should have had a becoming rosy complexion, but I didn't – I was contrastingly pale.

I think the best thing that could be said of my features was that they were regular and in proportion and I had a good set of white, even teeth, and was occasionally accused of having a "nice smile", but I don't think I could ever have been considered a head turner.

Dancing was one of my favourite forms of entertainment and we often went to the Saturday night 'hops' together, which were held in the Village Hall, or the Church Hall – whichever was available. Unsurprisingly, Denise was always the one who had the pick of the good-looking men to dance with, whilst I was sometimes grateful to have *anyone* ask me to dance. I remember on one occasion admiring Denise as she effortlessly floated around the floor in the arms of some handsome man; how envious I felt and wished I was doing the same. It was not a good feeling to be sitting there decorating the wall. In fact, so desperate was I to have someone ask me to dance, that after a quick look round, I got up and went to sit next to the plainest girl in the vicinity, in the hope that I might show up well against her. She was overweight, had lank, greasy hair, heavy features and spots on her chin. Shortly, a very presentable young airman advanced across the floor towards where we were sitting and as he got nearer I was already half-way onto my feet to smilingly accept his invitation to dance. I couldn't believe it when he ignored me and took the hand of the ugly girl beside me.

After this humiliating experience, I decided that I didn't much like men and they'd got no taste anyway. Also, I'd had a few unfortunate skirmishes with men in the past, whose sole aim seemed to be to want to scrape my tonsils and try to ravish my body before I'd even got to know their name, or they mine and I wasn't having any of that! I cherished the unrealistic notion that it would be the romantic, tender love I read about in novels or nothing. It was mostly nothing.

So I lavished all my devoted, if undeclared love and admiration on Denise, without any thought of reciprocal feelings. It was enough just to be in her company.

We sometimes went out in a foursome, but there being little else to do in the winter months in this quiet town, we would occasionally go to a pub. The first time this happened, I'd never been in a public house before and I was ignorant of what to ask for.

'I'll have a bee-ar,' said Denise.

'I'll have a bee-ar too,' I echoed, thinking this sounded awfully sophisticated, and what was good enough for her would certainly be good enough for me.

'Pint or a half? Mild or Bitter?'

'Pint of Bitter please,' came the reply, so again, I echoed her order.

I had no idea what a pint of Bitter looked like, much less how awful it tasted. The first sip was such a disappointment. It lingered on my palate like poison and tasted a bit like the dose of Senna Pods we were forced to drink on a Saturday morning at St. Anne's to keep us regular, and my heart sank at the daunting thought of having to drink the whole pint. Denise seemed to have no problem at all and kept up with the men, but nothing would induce me to have another drink, struggling, as I was, to get the revolting liquid I already had down my throat. I resolved that if ever I went in a pub again, I would ask for a nice, safe, sweet tasting bottle of Vimto - much more in accordance with my simple tastes.

We got up to leave and I was surprised to discover that I felt light-headed and stupid with legs that had a mind of their own. Denise linked her arm through mine and we giggled our way back to the hotel where we were billeted. She led me up to the room we shared, slowly undressed me, then slipped into my narrow bed beside me.

This was the first of many nights we spent together but our affair didn't last. When I was nineteen, I went to RAF Halton to do a six month course to become a Physical Training Instructor and whilst I was away Denise got posted to RAF Stranraer in Scotland and we never saw each other again.. It was a short-lived and unconventional romance, but looking back, one of the most beautiful experiences of my life.

Chapter 24

Physical Jerks and a Ring.

When I returned to my RAF station in Sidmouth it was as a qualified physical training instructor which carried an automatic promotion to that of Corporal. I had been issued with a complete set of P.T.I. kit and fancied myself particularly in the lovely white, woollen rollneck sweater and tiny flared skirt which I wore with pride as often as my duties permitted.

But although I was fit and looked the goods, I was a bit disappointed to discover that I didn't seem nearly as popular with my colleagues in my new role as I had been when I worked as a clerk. For most people didn't seem to share my enthusiasm for fitness, much less being made to indulge in physical jerks, and some even reported sick complaining that I'd worked them too hard and made their limbs stiff and painful. In my initial enthusiasm to get everyone fit, I failed to realise that people were far short of my fitness level, and that putting them through a series of rigorous exercises probably did them more harm than good. So there was great rejoicing when I got a prolonged spell of laryngitis and was unable to speak beyond a squeak for at least three weeks. When I resumed duties I moderated my enthusiasm and arranged my physical training schedule so that it was more commensurate with the general fitness and limited ability of the reluctant participants. I think we reached a happy compromise in the end.

Things began to liven up considerably in Sidmouth when we had an invasion of American soldiers and sailors, who were stationed at Slap Sands, near Sidmouth, where I now realise they were in training for the D- Day landings in Normandy on June 6th 1944. We knew there was something momentous afoot, but no one knew exactly what, until it happened. In the meantime, we were pleased to become the temporary girl friends of these handsome, well fed, and extremely generous Americans, who brought us all manner of goodies, including oranges, chocolate, make-up and nylon stockings.

I became friendly with a naval officer called Brad and his mate Stanwick. They asked me if I had a friend to make a foursome, so I asked my friend Jean if she would like to come along. At the given date and time I was disappointed when only Stan turned up, and when I asked where Brad was, he explained that there had been a training accident at sea, and Brad had been killed. Jean went off on the date with Stan whilst I went back to my room to ponder on the fate of poor Brad, so young, so handsome, and so healthy. It seemed so tragic to think of all the young men who died in the best of health. It wasn't until after the war that I learned that in the so-called 'accident at sea' the boat had been in a training position prior to the invasion of Normandy, but due to lack of proper communication, it had been torpedoed by a German U-boat, with the loss of 946 lives.

Stefan Kopervas, the Czech soldier, had kept in touch and he sometimes came to Sidmouth to see me when he was on leave. He was good looking in a swarthy sort of way, with a lot of dark wavy hair and wide apart, deep set brown eyes. He must have been at least ten years older than me and for all I knew, he could already have a wife and family in his native Czechoslovakia, so I was surprised when, on his embarkation leave, he turned up with an engagement ring and asked me to marry him. I didn't want to hurt his feelings by turning him down flat, so tried to soften the refusal by saying it would be more sensible to wait until after the war. He persuaded me to take the ring anyway, which fitted and looked nice, so I didn't need too much persuading to accept it. It was late when I got back to my billet and so as not to disturb my room mate, I crept in very quietly and did not put a light on.

She whispered, 'It's all right, I'm not asleep, have you had a nice time?'

'Yes thank you,' I whispered back, 'I got engaged.'

'What!' she shouted, and before I knew it, the lights were on and she shot up from her bed demanding to see the ring.

I expected her to be pleased for me, instead of which, she looked at me with a measure of concern clouding her features and quietly said, 'Do you think this is right for you?'

'Perhaps not,' I said with shrug.

It was a five day wonder. I never heard from Stefan again. I could only imagine that he'd gone on the D-Day Landings, along with servicemen from many parts of the world who had taken part in the invasion. So many never came back.

Out of sheer sentiment, I still have his photograph to this day, along with photos of other men friends I'd collected over the years. It was quite the thing in those days to have a studio photograph taken in uniform, and in too many cases, it would be all the wives, girl friends or parents of these young men would have to remind them of their missing loved ones.

Chapter 25

The End of Hostilities.

Looking back, I find it strange that when peace was declared in Europe in May 1945 I remember nothing at all about any celebrations, although I'm sure there must have been some where I was now stationed at RAF Halton. I do remember a profound sense of relief that the conflict was now over, but this was mingled with an entirely selfish emotion. I was happy in my work, I'd made lots of friends in the WAAF and best of all, I had become a different person - more confident, more sure of myself, and unburdened with the old, soul disfiguring trappings of my former life. Was it now all to end with the ending of hostilities?

The answer wasn't long in coming. A few months previously, the RAF had asked for volunteers in certain trades in the WAAF to serve in India, so one of my friends and I applied for the posting. But with the war being over I thought that would be that. However, we were advised that if we were prepared to sign on for a further twelve months we could be considered for a posting to the Middle East.

So I, together with about forty other girls from various RAF stations throughout the country, underwent a rigorous medical examination to assess our physical fitness and were then tested on our mental alertness and quizzed on our standards of morality. The worst part of the medical for those of us who were passed fit was when we had to line up, in alphabetical order, to be inoculated against the multitude of diseases we could pick up in a foreign country. It wouldn't happen now, but in the less enlightened days of the 1940's, the same needle was re-filled and used to inject all of us, and as I was towards the end of the alphabet, it was always blunt by the time it was my turn. Having sinewy, finely muscled arms, it was difficult enough to get the needle in anyway, but at least we girls bravely stood our ground, whilst the men were fainting all over the place. It never occurred to the medics or us that while protecting us against foreign diseases, they might well be injecting us with someone else's disease. Anyway, we none of us seemed any the worse for the experience.

We were given lectures on how to behave; it being pointed out that we were, in a way, ambassadors for our country, and our behaviour would reflect Britain's good name or otherwise. We were also warned of the dangers of unsuitable sexual alliances, and reminded that if anyone was irresponsible enough to find themselves pregnant whilst abroad and gave birth there, then the child would have to take the nationality of the country in which it was born. (I don't know how far true this might be today, but it certainly gave one something to think about). We were also told that if any male member of the forces laid an unwanted finger on us – well – there was still a war going on in the Far East.

With these dire warnings and admonishments seared into our souls, we set sail from Southampton to Algiers in July 1945. I remember little about the journey except that I was sea sick all the way. It was a bit ironic really, that I, on my way overseas to keep others fit, should be the one to succumb to sea sickness and I admit I felt a bit of a failure as I spent most of the journey lying like a lazy dog on the deck.

Chapter 26

North Africa

Service life was very different abroad. Discipline was relaxed, there was no obligatory morning roll call and the only enforced physical activity was that imposed by me. Due to the suffocating heat, I limited physical jerks to 30 minutes in the morning for the women, followed by 30 minutes for the men, with the occasional hockey or cricket match against the Navy or the Army thrown in for good measure. We mostly had to play mixed matches as there weren't enough women to make up a full team, so things could get quite scary at times, especially when a hockey ball came scudding towards your shins at a hundred miles an hour. We got swellings on our unprotected shins as big as eggs, but I never saw anyone rolling around on the ground in agony. We just winced, gave our wound a quick rub and got on with it.

We had only one WAAF Officer who was supposed to be in charge of us, but I think she had a bit of a problem communicating with people, for I never knew her to have a proper conversation with anyone. Whether it was because she didn't think it right and proper to hold conversations with "other ranks" I don't know, but other than male officers, who didn't seem much interested in her, there wouldn't be anyone else with whom she could speak.

I remember one occasion when we invited the Navy hockey team to join our hockey team for a celebratory meal at a local hotel. As a matter of courtesy, we invited her to join us. She sat next to me, but even though the conversation was flowing as freely as the wine, she spoke hardly a word, despite my attempts to be as pleasant as I knew how and draw her out, but she would not respond. Presently, a dog sauntered into the dining room and began foraging between our legs for any dropped scraps of food. Someone threw it a bone.

She glared in undisguised horror at the bone-thrower, who smiled charmingly back, then fixed her disapproving stare on the dog. As often happens during a noisy gathering, save for the clacking of knives and forks on plates, there happens a collective lull in the conversation. It was broken when she pronounced, in a loud, ululating voice:

'It's simply amazing with what extraordinary rapidity that minute dog devoured that enormous bone.'

She never spoke another word until it was time to leave, when she announced what a splendid evening she'd had.

One Sunday morning, shortly after arriving in Algiers, a truck load of American soldiers turned up at the hotel in which we were billeted to see if we girls would like to go to the beach. Some of us said we would (better a sea breeze than the oppressive heat of the city) so we clambered into their transport and off we went.

There was no sea breeze and very little shade, but some of the girls shed their clothing and happily cavorted about in their bathing costumes, either swimming or sunbathing - but not I. Despite my athleticism and natural ability to play games, the one thing I could not do was swim. Also, being fair skinned, I was anxious not to expose my body to the burning sun, or the critical gaze of my companions.

So although I got into a bathing costume, I sat in the shade of a hot rock, wrapped loosely in a large towel for most of the time, chatting to one of the soldiers who seemed reluctant to leave my side. He was tall, tanned and rugged, said his name was Hank, and spoke with a lazy, Southern drawl. He told me all about his family in America adding proudly that his father was a police chief. I listened with polite interest but refused to be impressed.

Admittedly, Algeria was perhaps a bit behind Europe with all its mod-cons but he seemed to think that North Africa was how the rest of the world lived outside America.

Having failed to impress me with his illustrious family, he droned on with another line-shooting gambit.

'Why in America we all have ice-cool fridges.'

'So have we!' I retorted.

'We've also got electric dish washers.'

'So have we!'

'We also have washing machines and electric vacuum cleaners.'

'Gosh! I am *so* impressed,' I said with a hint of sarcasm, then added, 'You do boast rather a lot though, don't you Hank.'

'Why honey, we sure do have something to boast about.'

There was no answer to that – so I didn't give one.

Despite his boastfulness, I did meet up with him a few times, mainly because it was considered too dangerous for us girls to go out in the evening without a male escort. As in Algiers, they were required to come to the Guard Room and sign for us, then bring us back safely to camp when we would be signed in. So for the time being, he served a useful purpose. But there was only so much boring boastfulness human flesh could stand, and the time came when I decided to sever the relationship. I was surprised at his reaction. Despite his manly appearance and brash, bragging nature, he cried and through his tears said, 'Why Honey, when I first see-d your lily-white limbs, ah said to *marself*: That girl's *gonna* be *ma* wife.'

How strange, I thought, when I'd always believed my pale skin the least desirable of any physical attributes I might possess. There's no accounting for taste.

Once we'd got ourselves properly settled in, camp dances and entertainments were organised, and, unlike in the U.K. there were at least ten men to every woman, which was quite a novelty at first, but the novelty soon began to pall after having our feet trampled on by men falling over themselves in their stampede to grab a girl.

We were transported to the dances in military trucks and no matter what, were obliged to stay until the end, having no other means of getting back to camp. On one occasion I said to my friend, Molly, 'I'm tired and I've had enough of this. I think I'll sit in the truck until it's time to go."

'I'll come with you,' she said. 'I have had enough too.'

I made use of the waiting time and rolled my hair up in pins. Then I took cleansing tissues from my handbag and wiped my make-up off, after which I plastered my face liberally in Ponds Cold Cream, all with a view to saving time when we got back to camp. Then we closed our eyes and sat quietly waiting for midnight when the dancing would be over..

It wasn't long before we were disturbed by men's voices and before we knew it, a couple of soldiers had climbed on board.

'Go away,' I said sharply. 'We've come out here for a bit of peace, not to be pestered by you!'

Either too drunk or too ignorant to take heed of what I was saying, they advanced upon us and tried to get amorous. One of them had a broad Yorkshire accent, and ignoring my protests, advanced upon me with the endearing words, '*Yer* not very *narce* looking, but you'll do for me.'

'Well *you* certainly won't do for me!' I spat indignantly. 'Now, get off this truck or I'll report you to the Military Police.'

Molly was outraged on my behalf and made me feel a bit better when she said, 'I wouldn't care – but it isn't even true!' I've never liked men with a Yorkshire accent ever since.

There were two young airmen who sometimes came to the dances who were nice looking, solicitous, polite, and who danced quite beautifully, but who never tried to make a pass, or even make a date with us other than saying, 'See you next Saturday.'

We were pleased, if a little puzzled, that their only interest in us was dancing, and concluded they were probably married, or had girl friends back home – which was fine.

The explanation was a bit more interesting than this, as I was to find out after they were posted back to the U.K. My role as a P.T.I. didn't occupy me all day every day, so in between times I worked in the office, part of my remit being to check all service documents of personnel who'd been posted, before forwarding them on to their new unit. Naturally, I took particular interest in the documentation of these two airmen and was shocked to discover they were both being treated for a venereal disease; which, according to the questionnaire, in each case was caught from a *professional.* Although this information was supposed to be strictly confidential, I couldn't wait to pass it on to Molly and was gratified to see her shocked reaction.

Sergeant Molly Mainwaring worked in the Admin office and her boss, Flight Lieutenant Eddie Mountford was the station adjutant. She and I had become really good friends. There was an indefinable something between us that needed no utterance, but which found expression in little acts of mutual caring, sharing of confidences, and giving of little presents.

One day she confessed she'd fallen in love with her boss, but knew it was a lost cause, for it was forbidden for Officers and Other Ranks to mix socially on a personal level. I said he probably felt the same about her, but for the same reason was unable to tell her so.

It was shortly after our conversation that the Commanding Officer – Group Captain Alan Simmonds – summoned me to his office. I knew him reasonably well on a workday level and he often joined in my physical jerks classes, mixed hockey matches etcetera, so I assumed this is what he wanted to discuss with me.

I knocked, entered, and gave the obligatory salute, before being invited to sit down.

'Now, Lynn' he said, 'I expect you're wondering why I've sent for you.'

Did I hear aright – did he *really* call me 'Lynn' instead of Corporal.

'Yes Sir.' I said, 'Is it about the cricket match against the Navy next week?'

He leaned back in his chair and studied me for a while before answering and I found myself thinking that I'd have arranged my hair nicely and put some make-up on had I known I was going to be under scrutiny.

He then put his right hand to his face, separated his fore and middle fingers between his top and lower lip as if to imply I shouldn't be saying this really, before answering my question.

'Well, it is about the match in a way, but I wondered if you would like to make up a foursome afterwards and go for a meal to The Safir Hotel?'

'That would lovely – thank you Sir,' I said, 'but may I ask who's making up the foursome?'

'Flt.Lt. Eddie Mountford and your friend Sgt. Mainwaring – er - Molly.'

'That will be lovely,' I said, struggling not to look too pleased and enthusiastic. 'Thank you Sir.'

When I left his office I took wings and floated off to see Molly and give her the good news. We almost collided, for at the same time she was on her way to tell me the glad tidings. I was much more thrilled for her than I was for myself – for even though I was immensely flattered by the invitation from someone in such an exalted position, I couldn't truthfully say I'd harboured any secret ambitions to be particularly noticed by him. He must have been at least twenty years older than me and I guessed he was probably married, but under the circumstances it didn't matter. I considered my part as probably a means to an end and was happy to go along with it.

It was Molly's birthday the night we went out for the meal and mine a few days later, so we had lots to celebrate and it turned out to be a wonderful evening. We met up most weekends after that and because they had access to military jeeps we were taken to all manner of interesting places. I liked going up into the mountains best, which were always cool and covered in snow, even though the sun would be shining from a clear blue sky and it would be hot as hell at sea level. We often took picnics with us and although it would appear that we had this mountainous white world to ourselves, we soon learned that this was not so. After finishing our picnic we threw the discarded left-overs into the snow for the birds. But it wasn't birds who came to claim them but a couple of Arabs who materialised from nowhere. They carefully placed the scraps in the hoods of their garments, presumably to take home for their families. They at least had the manners to keep out of sight until we'd finished eating and on any subsequent trips, I always made sure I discarded at least as much as I ate. We stopped going up to the mountains when Alan was laid low with a bout of mountain sickness and there was nothing to be done about it except to get off the slopes with all haste.

There were other times when, on the excuse that their serviceability needed to be checked, we would be taken on board an air/sea rescue launch for a spin round the coast. I was a bit dubious about this at first, thinking I might disgrace myself by becoming sea sick, but to my relief, it never happened and I was able to enjoy the experience, although we never had the thrill of actually having to rescue anyone.

This was the good life, and I sometimes wondered what I'd done to deserve all this happiness. I loved my job and I loved my friends and I especially loved Molly with her quiet ways and gentle humour, and my admiration for her was no doubt influenced by the fact that she seemed to like me too.

Alan told me he was married about the second time we went out and I was pleased, as I couldn't say I fancied him, neither was I looking for an affair, so we kept our relationship on a purely platonic basis, which suited me fine. I enjoyed the kudos of being *thought* his girlfriend and the pleasure of his company and all that went with it without any strings.

However, things seldom stay the same forever and soon there were to be many changes. There had been rumblings in Algeria by the indigenous Arab population against the French, who then ruled the country. The British Government feared there would be an uprising, possibly leading to a civil war, so it was decided to get us women out of North Africa with all haste.

I was pleased when Molly confided in me that Eddie had asked her to marry him after she was demobbed. We hugged, and for the first and only time, kissed each other on the lips. We looked into each others eyes, then I turned away. Was that a tear I saw spilling down her cheek or was it perspiration from the intense heat? For my own peace of mind I preferred not to know.

Molly went back to England, got demobbed and married Eddie and eventually they had two lovely children. I was sent to Egypt to serve out the rest of my time there and as it happened, the anticipated uprising didn't happen in Algeria for several more years, although there were minor skirmishes breaking out somewhere or other all the time. This was not surprising for the French treated the Arabs abominably, even to the point of officially designating themselves as *citizens* whilst the Arabs were given the lower status of *subjects* and were not even allowed a vote.

There was food and clothing rationing in force, but only for the French. The Arabs were not given entitlement to anything and had to rely on their wits, begging, stealing and bartering to get anything at all. They had money because they worked for it, but had nothing on which to spend it; so they would pay us handsomely for anything we had a mind to sell them, such as soap, fags, chocolate or whatever. We didn't get robbed at our living and sleeping quarters as we were safely housed in an hotel with guards posted at the entrance, but I do remember an occasion when some of us (happily I was not one of the 'us') got robbed in a very unique way. We were on our way, in open military transport, to another part of Algiers, to attend a course on something or other. We sat on the benches whilst our kit bags were piled up around us. I wondered why a couple of Arabs were standing at the side of a road holding, what looked like, fishing rods. As we drew near, they expertly flicked out their rods and hooked out a couple of kit bags. By the time we'd recovered our wits and alerted the driver to stop, the "fishermen" were away on their toes and nothing to be done. I thought this a clever and ingenious way of relieving us of our property, but might not have felt quite the same if it was my bag that had been lifted.

Not only were the Arabs denied the basic necessities of life, but they were also treated as less than human by the French. I remember once watching some Arab labourers working on a building construction with a French Foreman in charge. The Foreman grabbed a wooden trestle and raised it high above his head. What a strange thing to do, I thought, and was then shocked to see him bring it down on the head of one of the Arabs. He fell to the ground and when one of his workmates bent over to help, he received a hefty kick up his backside which sent sprawling. I ran to our medical section and asked them to tend to the injured Arabs. They cleansed and bound up the bleeding wound on the head of the one, but nothing could be done for the one who'd been kicked except murmurs of sympathy, the while the Foreman gesticulated and wildly protested.. The incident became less fraught when one of the WAAF medics sensibly produced three cups of tea, handing the first one to the Frenchman. Now who could continue to be angry after a nice friendly gesture like that?

Afterwards, I spoke to one of the French women who worked for us and said how dreadful I thought it was. A pleasant, ordinary young lady, she looked at me in surprise, turned up the palms of her hands and with a slight shrug said, 'It does not matter – *zey* are only Arabs.'

.

Chapter 27

Egypt

We sailed from Algiers to Port Said, when I was again laid low with seasickness, and were then taken by road to an RAF desert location on the outskirts of Heliopolis, Cairo. I was tired and feeling like death when we were dropped off at the guardroom, from where we had to walk some distance in the searing heat, carrying our heavy luggage. I heaved my kit bag onto my shoulders and with a suitcase in my hand began the trudge to our tented accommodation. I hadn't got far before I had to stop and rest, and finally succumbed to the persistent pleadings of one of the locals to carry my bags. But before he would budge he demanded, 'You pay me first.'

I foolishly paid him, so grateful was I to be relieved of my burden, but we hadn't got very far when he stopped and dumped my luggage. I thought he wanted a rest and I was glad to stop too, until he demanded, 'You give me more money or I not carry.'

I argued but he wouldn't budge, so I gave him more money and this pattern repeated itself a few more times, so that by the time we got to my destination, my meagre purse was practically empty. Apart from the heat, the headache and the weariness, I was also feeling very cross with myself for being too feeble to carry my own bags and for allowing myself to be so easily duped. I soon learned.

It was a bit of a culture shock to see where I was to spend the next six months of my life. The tents were fairly large and were erected over a concrete base, surrounded by a low rectangular wall with two concrete steps down to enter. The furnishings were sparse and consisted of three small beds, three bedside lockers and three large, metal, coffin-like lock-up boxes which were housed beneath the beds and in which we had to keep everything, including clothing and valuables. At some distance from the tents there was a purpose built brick structure which contained a row of toilets, washbasins and showers from where we drew our drinking water. In the opposite direction was another large, brick building where we worked, ate, socialised and had our being.

I shared a tent with two others – Cpl. Kay Baldy (known familiarly as Baldy) and Cpl. Cynthia Lyle and it was fortunate that, sleeping in such a confined area and in such primitive conditions, we got on very well together. The tents *did* have electric lighting, which was just as well as there were no softly creeping crepuscular evenings here. Darkness descended early and rapidly, but at least we were able to read, play cards or just socialise in the artificial light, dim though it was. Almost as easily as I'd accustomed myself to living in hotels in agreeable places in England and Algiers, I now adjusted to our new, primitive living conditions, although I found the occasional sand storms pretty hard to bear, especially when our tents were flattened to the ground and hot sand whipped into hair, eyes, nose and mouth.

We were allowed to go out in the day time without having to have a male escort to sign for us, which was nice, but we were advised not to wear uniform as we would be easily identifiable as 'British' and it seemed the Egyptians didn't like us very much. However, we got on well with those who worked for us and with whom we had close contact. It was the opposite from Algeria, where we women had *always* to wear uniform so that we wouldn't be mistaken for the French.

By contrast with the deprivations and shortages in Algiers and Britain, Egypt, or at least Cairo, seemed like a land of plenty, with the shops crammed with all manner of exciting merchandise, including exotic food, fancy goods and clothes. The hotels were large and luxurious and the exotic cafes served iced coffee and a mouth watering selection of cakes and pastries, the only restriction on indulging in all these goodies being the cost.

But Egypt, although a seeming land of plenty, was mainly for those who had plenty, for it was also a land of massive contrasts between those who were obscenely rich and those who were exceedingly poor, with only a thinly scraped layer of the bourgeois in between.

I loved the bazaars and markets, my favourite being Peanut Alley and it didn't take me long to realize that one was never expected to pay the original asking price for anything, and I quickly became an expert at bargaining. I remember striking a hard bargain over a leather hold-all, and was amused to be told by the Arab stall holder, 'Och, you're a hard case Jock.'

Another expression often used during bargaining, and which always made me smile was, 'Queen Victoria – very nice lady.'

I used to send Muriel small gifts and was always pleased to have letters from her giving me her news. She was now sixteen and had left St. Anne's Home. Due to changing attitudes and social conditions, it was no longer the practice for children to be sent out to work as domestic servants, so she was working as a telephonist at the G.P.O. and living in a tiny bed sitting-room. I recall one of her letters telling me that it was so cold when she was walking to work that her eyelashes froze. As I read the letter I was so hot the sweat trickled down my forehead into my eyes and made them sting, and I remember thinking: Gosh – how marvellous. I wish I was cold.

It was really too hot to do much in the way of physical training, so apart from organising the odd cricket, tennis or hockey matches, my work was now mainly concerned with welfare and administration and the occasional so-called Guard Duty, which necessitated sitting in the Guard Room all night, checking that those who'd signed out were duly signed back in again on their return, and waiting for something untoward to happen which, to date and to my knowledge, hadn't. So after midnight, I would spend most of the time nodding off.   We had men from the RAF Regiment with guard dogs supposed to be patrolling the perimeters of the camp anyway, so *they* would know if there was anything alarming going on.

However, there was one Saturday night when I was very lucky indeed to be on guard duty. Several WAAF had been taken in a military transport truck to another RAF Station to a dance, and were it not for the fact that I was on duty, I might well have been with them.

In the event, I was sitting in the guard room around midnight, fighting off the desire to sleep, and waiting for them to return so that I could sign them safely in, and then get back to intermittently nodding the rest of the night away. Midnight came and went and still no sign of anyone and at one o'clock in the morning I was speculating as to what might have happened to them when my reverie was disturbed by the ringing of the telephone. The distressed voice on the end of the line said there had been a serious motor accident and could I send help. I was given sketchy details of the nature of the accident and after establishing where it had happened, I phoned the station medical officer, who rushed to the scene with a couple of ambulances in tow. I waited anxiously to know what the injuries were, if anyone had been taken to hospital and to check the non-injured back into camp. It was much worse than I could have imagined.

It transpired that after the dance was over, the girls were waiting in the transport to be driven back to camp, but the official RAF driver, for whatever reason, failed to turn up, so another airman, who had no right to be driving and whom it transpired, was drunk, took the keys, got into the truck and drove off. According to the passengers, the vehicle was being driven fast and erratically and ultimately, it turned over.

Several of the girls sustained injuries, some very serious, and one girl whose name I've forgotten, lost an arm. This was bad enough, but I spent the rest of the night in stunned grief when I learned that Irene, a close friend of mine, had been killed. She was a beautiful girl, and had a lovely personality to go with her good looks. It was only the previous afternoon, when we were suffering the oven hot heat of a sirocco wind, that she made a strange, but in retrospect, almost prophetic remark: 'Phew!' she said, as she genteelly dabbed at the freely flowing perspiration on her brow, 'If I should die, I hope they put me in a cool grave.' She was buried the very next day in the blistering heat.

Chapter 28

The Compassionate Thief.

It was not an uncommon occurrence for the camp to be raided at night and any possessions not locked away in the large, heavy boxes were likely be stolen. So stealthy were the raiders that often we wouldn't know we'd been robbed until the morning. Sometimes, people even had their blankets taken off their beds without them knowing, until they woke up shivering, for although the days were unbearably hot, the nights were always very cold.

It happened one night to me and my fellow tent sharers, Baldy and Cynthia. I woke up and knew we were being burgled, but I kept quiet, not daring to move a muscle which might indicate that I was awake. I did eventually open half an eye, just in time to see two Arabs leaving the tent with whatever they could lay their hands on. As soon as they were gone, as if by a given command, we all three shot up in our beds and simultaneously cried out: 'We've been robbed!' It seems we'd all been awake, and all had the same thoughts on self-preservation, deeming our lives to be more important than our possessions.

This was a night raid and several other tents had had a similar experience, although most of the occupants had slept through it.

There was another occasion which was even more alarming for me. It was day time and the camp was almost deserted. Being a Bank Holiday, most of my colleagues and friends had gone off to spend the week-end in Jerusalem or some other place of their choice.

I lay on my narrow bunk in the tent, alternatively shivering and burning in the searing heat of the desert sun, racked with the pain in my head so intense that even the slightest movement was enough to send rivers of agony roaring through my head.

Inch long black spiders scuttled around on the concrete base of the tent, whilst others sucked on the porous water pitcher that stood on the two foot high wall surrounding the base and over which the tent was pitched. Marauding, hateful, stinging, invasive creatures, brazenly scurrying around in my space would normally be slain without mercy, but today they were left unmolested. I could only watch their seemingly mindless to-ing and fro-ing and even envy those that were slaking their thirst on the life giving water seeping through the cooling pitcher; water which I craved but was too enfeebled to reach.

I had planned to go with my friends to Jerusalem, but the day before I'd played an inter-service cricket match, foolishly, without any head protection in the fierce heat of the Egyptian sun, after which, I began to feel very unwell. This was particularly annoying as, being a physical training instructor, it was my job to keep people fit, instead of which I had rendered myself very unfit.

So I told my friends to go ahead without me and assured them I would try and cadge a flight the next day and join them at St. David's Hotel in Jerusalem. This was a popular venue with Service personnel until it was blown up by the so called Jewish Stern Gang, who, at the time, were waging guerrilla warfare against the hated British.

After my friends left I didn't, as I had hoped, feel any better. In fact I felt much worse. There were times when I was delirious and others when I seemed to drift in and out of consciousness, only to be brought back to reality by another surge of excruciating pain. As I lay there suffering in the suffocating heat, to add to my discomfort and feeling of nausea, I became aware of the pungent smell of garlic. Can I really smell garlic, I wondered or is it the imagination of my fevered brain. Then, a brief, visceral stab of fear shot through me as I realised that I was not alone. I hadn't seen or heard a thing but, rigid with fear, I slowly steeled myself to roll my eyes to the left. Was I hallucinating, or was that a white robed Arab across the other side of the tent? I soon realised he was real when I saw him calmly stuffing our belongings into the kit-bags lying at the foot of the empty beds. I watched, not daring to breathe or move a pain-racked muscle. Then I recalled that, after the previous night raid, I'd taken the precaution of keeping a hockey stick at the right hand side of my bed and a whistle on my locker for just such an occasion as this. But I had neither the strength nor ability to use them, and who was there to hear my whistle anyway?

When the intruder had put everything he could lay his hands on into the kit bags, he made towards the open flaps of the exit and I breathed an imperceptible sigh of relief that he was finally on his way out. I was wrong. He dropped the bags at the opening, then, almost as an after thought, turned his head and made his way over to where I lay. I closed my eyes feigning sleep, hoping he'd think I hadn't seen or heard him, but the smell of garlic grew stronger and I could feel his breath on my face. I slowly opened my eyes to find him looking down at me and I looked back. Feeling too ill to show anger or fear, I wondered whether he was going to relieve me of my bedding, rape me, murder me or all three. Given the agony I was in, I felt murder might be the most merciful thing, provided he did it very quickly, like a stab to the heart or the jugular.

His face gradually came into focus and I got the fleeting impression that he looked more scared than threatening and certainly not as evil as his garlic-laden breath suggested, odiously unpleasant though it was.

Then I found myself muttering through parched lips, 'Water. Water,' as I feebly raised a finger in the direction of the water pitcher. He fetched the pitcher, swiped the ants off it, (some of which fell on me) then put it to my lips. The water trickled down my throat and spilled over my face, then he poured the rest over my head. Slightly revived, I bravely asked him to fill the pitcher with more water, indicating the ablution building from where it could be obtained. He disappeared, but I knew he would come back for he'd left his loot behind.

When he returned, he put the pitcher down close to where I lay, darted me a swift look of pity, then softly stole away with his booty, leaving me with my bedclothes and honour intact and foolishly mouthing, 'Thank you. Thank you.'

My two tent sharers were none too pleased when they returned from their week-end and found me half dead and nearly all their belongings missing. I got the impression they were more concerned about their stolen items than the sorry state of my health, but to their credit, they got in touch with the medics immediately and I was taken to an RAF hospital to recover from what was diagnosed as severe sunstroke.

It 's almost seventy years since this alarming episode took place, and I have often thought of that mysterious intruder and wondered if he was real, or a delirium induced phantom of my imagination. Then I remember the reality of the stolen goods and the life-saving water and give thanks to providence for sending me a white-robed, guardian angel in the guise of a compassionate thief.

Chapter 29

Comparisons

In November 1946 my time in Egypt was up. Despite the tragic accident that killed one and maimed others of my friends; the occasional frightening personal experiences; the intense heat and the basic living arrangements, I enjoyed my time in Cairo and was sorry when it came to an end.

I liked the people too, for although officially, they did not like the British,, we got on very well with the men who actually worked for us doing the menial tasks such as serving meals, washing up, cleaning etcetera. I remember a conversation I had with the man who was cleaning my office. It was shortly after the road accident and I was feeling rather sorrowful.

'Why you sad?' he said.

Not wishing to enter into an explanation as to why I was feeling low, nor wanting to bare my soul to a stranger, I shrugged my shoulders and said dismissively, 'Just one of those things.'

He persisted, 'I not understand why you sad. You beautiful. You rich.'

I wasn't too sure about the *beautiful*, but I knew for certain I wasn't *rich*.

So I ignored the *beautiful* and smilingly said, 'I'm not rich.'

'You are rich,' he insisted. 'You have nice clothes, you have plenty food, you have bed, you are rich.'

It made me think: everything was comparative and by his and his compatriots' pitiable standard of existence – I *was* rich. I could have told him that wealth wasn't necessarily the key to perennial happiness, but I didn't because it would have been fatuous and patronizing. And I realised that whilst wealth was not necessarily the key to eternal happiness, grinding poverty could certainly contribute to everlasting misery.

It was commonplace for those waiting on us at table to swipe the discarded food from our plates and ram it into their mouths before consigning the crockery to the washing up bowl. Unmannerly and shocking as it seems, I could quite understand why they did it.

Even so, one had to be very cautious about showing sympathy or succumbing to the pleas for alms. Beggars were everywhere, and if you dropped a coin into the hands of one beggar, you would be besieged by a swarm of derelicts converging from all directions, all with genuine claims on your charity; the sad lesson being – if you can't give to all – give to none.

My life had been enriched immeasurably and in many ways. I'd sailed on the Nile; ridden Arab horses in the desert, marvelled at the Pyramids at Giza, dipped my toe in the Red Sea at El Sokhna and visited Jerusalem and other holy places of historical and biblical interest; but most precious, was the friendship and camaraderie I'd enjoyed during my time in the Forces and the increasing self-confidence I had gained over the last five and a half years, which had been some of the happiest of my life. Now, it was shortly to be all over.

I stood on the quayside at Alexandria chatting with my Service colleagues whilst we waited to board the ship that would take us back to the UK. An air of eager anticipation prevailed, which I pretended to share, but which, in truth, I was far from feeling. There was no eager looking forward to being welcomed home by partners, family or friends, only a vague sense of apprehension, mingled with a sliver of optimism.

Here I was, in the late autumn of 1946, twenty-two years of age, with no credentials to speak of but myself, on the threshold of a new life that had no known beginning.

Chapter 30

New Beginnings

After disembarking at Southampton I travelled north to RAF Wilmslow, where I was given my discharge papers and what pay was due, together with an extra small sum of rehabilitation money; and this, together with a little money I'd managed to save, was to ease my transition from Service life into the brave new world of the post war era in an almost bankrupt Britain.

I found myself sitting in the waiting room at Piccadilly Station, Manchester, wondering where I should take a train to. It was a raw November day and I was glad to be still wearing my uniform, for I had no winter clothes, the only clothing I had, other than my uniform, being the silken summer dresses I'd had made in Cairo and some flimsy summer sandals, of little use to me now. I shivered and hoped it wouldn't be too long before I could obtain my clothes rationing coupons to enable me to buy something more suitable for the British winter.

Whilst lingering over a cup of weak, sugarless tea in the station canteen, I tried to think positively about my future. I took my Service Book from my handbag and idly perused it, hardly a passport into *civvy street,* but practically my only credential. Apart from my number, rank and name, it recorded my civilian occupation on joining the WAAF, my length of service (five and a half years), a tick against the box which said: 'Highly satisfactory' for my work as a physical training instructor, and under the heading 'Character' a tick had been placed next to the option, 'Exemplary'.

I began to wonder if perhaps it would have been more prudent to have accepted one of the marriage proposals that occasionally chanced my way, but dismissed the thought almost as soon as it entered my head. Wherever my talents or skills might lie, I knew they were not in the bedroom.

Through the administrative side of my work, my office skills had been honed and improved during my time in the WAAF, so I felt that to try for a job in an office would be my best option, although in my optimistic more fanciful moments, I harboured thoughts about becoming a journalist. It would certainly be a step or two up from the domestic drudgery of my former existence. But where to go to find a job? Should I stay where I was and try to find a bed and breakfast for the night and start looking for a job the next day? I looked at the miserable, dreary streets around the station and dismissed the thought immediately. My mind went back to the small village in South Wales where I'd lived until I was ten, but I realised there would be nothing or no one there for me. Maybe I would go to London or Birmingham, where job prospects might be better, but then I dismissed the idea of being friendless and alone, and possibly jobless in a strange city.

When asked where I wanted my travel warrant made out to I'd said Leamington Spa, so that is where I would go. At least I knew the place and would be near to my sister, who was now sixteen, living in a bed-sit and working at the Post Office. All the other options that I'd briefly considered were mere idle musings.

When I arrived at Leamington Station in the late afternoon I didn't leave the platform immediately but sat in the waiting room where there was a nice coal fire burning and considered my next move. Should I start looking for somewhere straight away to spend the night, or should I wait where I was until it was time for Muriel to get back from work and go to see her first? I thought about St. Anne's Home and the day when Muriel and I had first arrived at this station all those years ago.

The present Matron – Mrs. Legge (formerly Miss Clifford) had been a junior member of the staff in my time there. Until Matey Powell's arrival, she was the only one who showed us any sympathy or understanding. We'd kept in touch over the years and she'd written to say I must be sure to go and see her when I got back to this country.

I decided to stay where I was for the time being, then go and see Muriel when it was time for her to get home from work. It felt strange and a little scary lugging my heavy baggage around. It contained everything I owned in the whole wide world, and I did not know where, or whether, I would find a destination for it.

An hour or so later, I left the comforting warmth of the waiting room and set off to find Muriel's address. It was a large house in a less salubrious part of the town, and I was quite taken aback when the door opened in response to my knock, and I found myself looking at a pretty young lady wearing make-up, with a bosom bigger than mine, in place of the child I'd left behind. It was lovely to see her after all this time, but the joy of our reunion was somewhat dampened when I saw the mean circumstances in which she was living. Her so-called 'bed-sit' was a tiny room about ten by ten feet with a bed, a hard wooden chair, a shabby chest of drawers, an even shabbier carpet, a gas ring on which to boil a kettle and do her cooking and a single bar electric fire. There must have been a cupboard for her food, but I don't remember seeing one. The bathroom and toilet facilities had to be shared with three other occupants, all middle-aged labouring men, plus, of course, the landlady. I didn't think this was suitable at all, but she said that accommodation was hard to find and this was all she could get for the rent she could afford. My heart sank.

For this evening at least, I decided, I would take her out for a meal at the nearby, modest establishment known as the Angel Hotel, where I also booked a double bedded room for the night. She told me how much things had changed at St. Anne's for the better, and how much more liberally minded the staff had become, especially since Mrs. Legge had been promoted Matron. No one was any longer forced to work as a domestic servant and the inmates of the Children's Homes were no longer defined as *Waifs & Strays* but were now known as the *The Children's Society*.

I gave her the presents I'd brought back for her, which included a silk scarf, a nightdress, and some silky underwear and a few souvenirs. She was thrilled, especially as clothing was still on ration in this country.

After breakfast the following morning, Muriel left to go to work and I made my way to the public library. It was warm and comfortable and familiar for I had spent many hours in the reading room here before joining up. The newspapers were free and I scrutinised the local ones for advertisements for jobs and accommodation. There were a few jobs advertised that I thought I might try for, but they required a written application to be submitted and this was no good – for I had no address to which a reply could be sent. There were a couple of advertisements under *Rooms to Let*, but if possible, I wanted to try and find something better than this so that Muriel and I could perhaps share a place. Feeling rather dispirited, I went to a phone box and telephoned Mrs. Legge to say I'd arrived back in this country and would it be all right if I called to see her. She seemed very pleased to hear from me and asked me to call straight away.

I couldn't have felt more welcome when I got there. She gave me a big hug, I gave her the present I'd bought her, and we talked about olden times over biscuits and coffee. She asked me where I'd stayed the night, and when I told her I'd booked into the Angel Hotel and would probably stay another night or so until I could find somewhere, she delighted me by saying, 'Don't do that. You can stay here until you find accommodation. It will only be a mattress in the attic, if you don't mind that.'

Of course I didn't mind. I could have cried with gratitude, but instead I just threw my arms about her and hugged her until the urge to weep passed. I met Muriel from work, told her my news, then we went to the hotel to spend one more night together.

Now that I had an address, I could write out applications for jobs, accommodation etcetera and after a few disappointments, I was accepted for a job as a clerk/typist at Sidney Flavells – a firm of gas cooker manufacturers, at a wage of £3.75 a week. A day or so later I received a reply to one of the many letters I'd sent out in response to the accommodation adverts, inviting me to a viewing. The house was in a nice part of town, and the accommodation on offer was a furnished bed/sitting room with separate kitchen and a shared bathroom and toilet on the same floor, but only one bath a week allowed. I could live with that. The rooms were clean, a reasonable size and adequately furnished and with the rent, at £1.50 per week, I felt I would be able to manage. Several applicants had been invited to view the place, so I was very pleased when it was offered to me.

Chapter 31

Making my way.

The transition into civilian life had not been too difficult after all, for I'd now found a job and somewhere to live in little over a week of arriving back in this country. How lucky could I get? I did have a few moments of anxiety after I'd moved into the bed-sit, when Mrs. Moss, the landlady, knocked on my door shortly after I'd moved in and challenged my trustworthiness. When I applied for the accommodation, I'd given 6, Warwick New Road, as my present address and Mrs. Legge as a reference, but I didn't think it necessary to mention it was a Children's Home and Mrs. Legge the matron.

She said, 'I've just got back from visiting the address you gave me and the person you gave as a reference. You didn't tell me it was a Children's Home. I wouldn't have let you have the flat if I'd known *that* was where you came from.'

I replied, politely and with what I hoped some dignity, 'If you think I'm less of a person for being an orphan Mrs. Moss, I'll leave at once and find somewhere else to live.'

She looked down at me beneath lidded yellow eyes and from her great height said haughtily, 'Oh, no need. You're here now, so you might as well stay I suppose, although I wouldn't have accepted you as a tenant had I known.'

I was aware how difficult it was to find somewhere to live, so I swallowed my pride and humbly thanked her and thought I would take my time over finding another billet. In the event, fifteen years later I was still there and still mindful that if I put a foot wrong or inadvertently displeased Mrs. Moss, she would, without any compunction, ask me to leave.

The winter of 1946/47, was quite the coldest I had experienced in my whole life, made the worse to bear after just coming back from living in a hot climate for one and a half years. The heating in the bed/sit was provided by a gas fire, but because the gas flow was restricted by what I understood were frozen pipes, the best flame I could get was about one inch, and if I tried to do any cooking all I would get was a tiny frill of blue round one gas ring and nothing in the fire, so it really was sometimes a question of heat or eat.

I got chilblains all over my toes and heels and getting my feet into my shoes in the morning and hobbling to work was an unbearable ordeal. But I was doing very well in my job, mainly probably, because I was willing to do a lot of voluntary, unpaid over-time, my un-stated reason being that it was more comfortable to sit in a warm cosy office than it was to shiver in my freezing home. If I didn't stay late in the office, Muriel and I would sometimes meet up after work and spend the evening in the reading room of the public library where we could keep warm until it was time to close.

Muriel was small, rounded and feminine, whilst I was slightly taller but slim and athletic. She had also discovered boys, whilst I'd spent most of my time discarding them. I'd begun to notice subtle changes in our attitude towards each other. It was no longer a little sister- big sister – or surrogate mother relationship. She had a mind of her own and was no longer the timid, biddable little girl I'd left behind. So despite my well intentioned aim of trying to find a flat which we could share, it was no surprise, indeed almost a relief, when, despite her dreary digs, she expressed no interest in my proposition. But we continued to see each other and I still worried about her and was pleased when, some months later, she told me she was going to live with a friend from work at her parents' house. I was even more pleased when I went to meet them and saw what a lovely home they had, and I knew she would be warm and safe. I solved the problem of heating my bed/sit when I found a one-bar electric fire in a second-hand shop and bought it for £1.

But when I confessed to Mrs. Moss what I'd done she promptly put the rent up to cover the extra cost of the electricity.

Mrs. Moss had a daughter – Kate - who was a house mistress at a girls boarding school. She came home for the school holidays and sometimes brought her friend – Miss Sankey – with her. Kate was a grey haired, middle-aged, well meaning but rather odd person, who, with her prissy manner and outdated ideas, did not seem to have developed much beyond the age of the pupils under her care. Miss Sankey was also a bit odd. She was unusually tall and imposing, yet with the look on her face of a startled fairy, which was at total odds with her general appearance. She was quietly spoken with a timid, retiring nature. One morning I was rudely awakened by a loud bang. I shot out of bed to investigate, opened the bathroom door across the landing from my room, and found a poor, bewildered Miss Sankey sitting, starkers on the edge of the bath, covered in soot from head to foot, looking very embarrassed and whimpering softly: 'Oh dear. Oh dear. I don't know what's happened.'

Kate Moss came rushing up from her quarters below stairs, and whilst she threw comforting arms round the simpering, sooted Miss Sankey, I did my best to explain what I thought had caused the explosion. I said the geyser was always a bit dodgy at the best of times, but because the gas pressure was so low the pilot light must have gone out, causing a leakage, hence the explosion when she tried to ignite it with a match. I don't think much notice was taken of my explanations, so concerned was Kate Moss with the unfortunate plight of her naked friend. There was no telephone in the house (only really posh people had one in those days) so I threw on some clothes and dashed out to call the Gas Board from a telephone kiosk. It took me a long time to pluck up enough courage to take my weekly bath after that

Chapter 32

Great Scott!

Mrs. Scott, who lived with her husband and young son in the flat above me, was also wary about taking a bath after that alarming episode.

Mrs. Janet Scott was a simple, nondescript, well intentioned little woman who had no ambition to be anything beyond that of being a good wife and mother. I became friendly with them and, never one to do much in the way of creative cooking, often donated the unused remnants of my weekly food ration to them. I also sometimes helped seven year old Billy with his homework if his father was on night shift or doing whatever else he did with his evenings. He belonged to the same county table tennis league as me and it was not unusual for us to leave the house together and get back at roughly the same time, both exhausted after an evening of strenuous activity.

However, Mrs. Scott's friendliness towards me cooled considerably when Billy announced one evening, 'Mum, I think you're the nicest *middle-aged* lady in the world.'

The smile of pleasure at this compliment from her precious boy froze on her lips when he added, 'And Miss Trowbridge is the nicest *young* lady in the world.'

Since she was only about three years older than me, his childlike declaration didn't go down too well, and I thought it judicious to spend less time in their company in future.

It wasn't long after this that her husband Norman and I happened to return to the house at the same time, after playing in a table tennis match, though not with or against each other. We chatted happily as we walked along and when we entered the house, we ascended the stairs together. I was about to open the door of my bed-sit when Mrs. Scott came charging down the stairs.

'I knew it! I knew it!' she shouted.

Taken aback, I said, 'Knew what?'

'Don't come the innocent with me,' she spat. 'You and Norman have been buzzing round each other like bees round a honey pot.'

I was shocked with the utter absurdity of her accusation and just stared at her in dumb amazement. Mindful that Mrs. Moss might be lurking in the hall listening to the conversation, I didn't even bother to refute her allegations before disappearing into my room and leaving Norman to deal with his wife's wild imaginings.

When I told Muriel about it she laughed and said, 'I can just imagine your reaction – eyes and mouth wide open in horror.'

I said I didn't think it was funny, but then I laughed too and thought no more about it. Even so, it was a bit of a relief when they moved shortly after this and I didn't see any of them again until years later, when a very handsome young man approached me at a function I was attending. Beaming broadly he put out his hand and said, 'Miss Trowbridge, how lovely to see you.'

It was Billy Scott and I was so pleased to see what a pleasant, personable young man he'd grown into.

Chapter 33

Lamentations

The next tenants of the flat above were an Irish couple, a Mr. & Mrs. O'Connell with a daughter about twelve called Carmel. He was a labourer at Fords factory and she worked in the canteen, and did freelance cleaning jobs at week-ends, between them earning enough money to send their daughter to a Catholic Boarding School. Both parents were semi illiterate and sometimes asked me to interpret official letters for them and, if necessary, write replies.

Mrs. O'Connell was given to lamenting and wailing loudly and I would often pop out onto the landing to listen, so fascinated was I by her laments. They have now passed into history and I can only clearly remember two. They were always prefixed with a prolonged 'Oh...Oh...Dear sacred heart of Jesus...' which was good, because it gave me fair warning that she was lamenting and I had time to get out and listen.

'Oh...Oh...Dear sacred heart of Jesus, 'tis a *fllty* pigsty *Oi'm* living in.'

She seldom had a response, but on this occasion her daughter said, 'Well mother, 'tis your *filty* pig sty. Get and clean it.'

Another lament I remember was when she once knocked on my door and said: 'Miss *Towbidge,* (she never pronounced the 'R's in my name) would you come up and have a cup of tea and take a look at this form we have to fill in?'

I agreed and went up shortly after to find Mrs. O'Connell up to her elbows in soap suds at the kitchen sink; Mr. O'Connell, recumbent in a chair with his legs spread before him and snoring very loudly and Carmel, obviously home on school holidays, with her head deeply in a book.

Mrs. O'Connell called to her daughter, 'Carmel, would you put the kettle on to make Miss *Towbidge* a cup of tea.' No response.

'Carmel!' she called again. 'Would you put the kettle on!' No response, the while I protested that I didn't really want a cup of tea.

Ignoring me, she screamed her request at Carmel once again, and when she still got no response, she furiously removed her hands from the washing, seized the plug of the kettle and rammed it into the socket. There was an almighty roar as her fat little body went flying backwards across the kitchen floor, causing her to bang her head on the kitchen cabinet, which in turn brought some of the crockery crashing to the floor.

She rubbed her head then wrung her hands and wailed, 'Oh... Oh... Dear sacred heart of Jesus, O*i'm* not worth tuppence after it!'

The wailing ceased momentarily to give her a chance to rant at Carmel, who remained calm and curiously unmoved. I picked up the broken crockery, which included a small china statue of the Virgin Mary. Fearing she might have an apoplectic fit if she realised the sacred mother of Jesus was no more, I quickly emptied the dustpan into the waste bin before she discovered the tragedy, then said, 'It wasn't really Carmel's fault. You could have killed yourself putting an electric plug into a socket with soaking wet hands.'

Another burst of wailing ensued.

'Oh...Oh... Dear sacred heart of Jesus, 'tis me own daughter *troi-ing* to kill me now.'

Mr. O'Connell stubbornly snored his way through the whole drama.

The family were ultimately given their marching orders, Mrs. Moss complaining they were too noisy and also dropped biscuit crumbs on the stairs. I was puzzled as to how this could have happened, but Mrs. Moss gave the unlikely explanation that they must have leaned over the banisters and brushed their clothes off after eating!

Chapter 34

Dangerous Deception

I lived in dread that I might inadvertently displease Mrs. Moss and be told to leave, and made my comings in and goings out as noiseless as possible, in case it brought the ever vigilant lady into the hallway. But despite my stealth, it never ceased to amaze me how often she managed to cross the hall from her sitting room at the front of the house to the dining room at the back, just as I was entering or leaving. She didn't actually ban male visitors, but strongly disapproved of them. I once overheard her remark to her long suffering husband: 'A short sharp walk would do them far more good!'

My chilblains were much too painful for "short sharp walks" and I had more than enough short sharp walking anyway getting to work and back. However, with the aid of pills and ointment, my chilblains eventually got better and I started going to dances on a Saturday night with friends from work. Here I met a nice looking chap called Reg who worked as a car mechanic. He was a good dancer (which went in his favour) and said he had a motor-bike and would like to take me for a spin sometime. I was not enthusiastic about this, it still being very cold and I didn't have any motorbike wearing attire. After a few more Saturday dates however, I did eventually allow myself to be persuaded to ride pillion, but having nothing suitable in my limited wardrobe, I wore my ordinary everyday clothes - tight skirt and high heels. Helmets were not obligatory in those days. Attired as I was, it was not easy to remain dignified when trying to mount the motorbike, and when I did get on, my skirt had risen well above my knees and resisted all tugging and attempts at trying to make myself look half decent. I was about to change my mind and say I didn't really want to do this, when Reg shouted 'Hang on,' then revved the engine and roared off. I threw my arms round his waist and pushed my body as tightly as I could into his back, but the wind whistled spitefully round my legs and up my skirt, and whipped my hatless, carefully combed hair into rats tails. To add to my discomfort, of all things, he had a pipe in his mouth and if he turned his head to the side, the ash from the pipe flew into my face. I was not in the least impressed, not even when he declared afterwards that I was a 'natural'.

Natural, I thought. What does he mean – natural - when I was feeling anything but natural, frozen to death as I was, and looking like Worzel Gummidge on a bad hair day.

It apparently had something to do with leaning into the bends instead of leaning in the opposite direction, unlike a lot of other girl pillion riders I was told. I wondered how many other girl pillion riders he'd had on his motorbike to compare me with, but said nothing, explaining only that any *leaning* I might have done was because I was hanging on to him for dear life and went whichever way his body took me. It was an experience I had no wish to repeat, at least not whilst the weather was so cold, so when he asked when he could see me again I told him I'd have to think about it and let him know. Reg was not to be easily brushed aside, and said he'd pick me up in a car for our next date.

March 1947 and winter had still not relinquished it's harsh, frozen grip on the country but when it did, it went out in a defiant, spectacular fury. Reg turned up in a posh Jaguar car for our next date. The weather was still pretty vicious but it didn't bother me for I would now be protected from the icy blasts and it was a novelty being whisked off to a country pub in such style and opulence, even if the beer shandy and packet of crisps hardly lived up to the style in which we'd arrived. It was still light when we emerged from the pub, but by now the gale force wind had increased in its ferocity, causing the trees to sway alarmingly. We had not travelled far when suddenly the car slewed to a halt. Reg screamed at me to get out and run. I thought he'd gone mad, but when he shouted again I didn't ask questions and tottered off as fast as my high heels and the slippery conditions would allow. Puffed, I stopped and looked back to see what I was running from. It was then that I saw that several telegraph wires had snapped and that a blown over tree was resting precariously on one single strand of wire, and Reg on his knees tugging furiously at the snapped wires that had become entangled in the nearside wheels of the car, which was obviously what had brought us to our untimely halt.

It was a great relief when he finally managed to disentangle the wires, and drove to where I was waiting, shivering with cold and fear. I scarcely had time to jump in and close the door before I heard a thundering crash and looked back to see the tree had fallen right on the spot where the car had stopped.

Reg was in a state, puffing and sweating and I noticed his hands were lacerated and bleeding. We drove on, and I told him how brave he was to do what he'd done but suggested it was a bit foolhardy to risk his life to save his car. He then shocked me by confessing it wasn't his car. It belonged to a customer who'd taken it to the garage for a service and he'd 'borrowed' it without permission.

This really was the end.

Chapter 35

Fickle Forays.

During my fickle forays into the *melange* of unsuitable dating, another incident springs to mind. Keith was slim, athletic, good looking and an excellent tennis player, so I was flattered when he asked if he could take me out. When the day arrived I rushed home from work and, anxious to look my best, forewent having a meal, choosing instead to have my once weekly allowed bath, after which I donned the best clothes before beginning to carefully apply my make-up. I was only part way through when the door bell rang. I went down the stairs to answer it, but did not switch on the landing light as I did not wish to be seen with only half a face on and my hair in rollers.

So I opened the door and without looking up said, 'You're early. I'm not ready yet. You'd better come in and wait.'

He followed me up the stairs and I shut him in the kitchen, then smiled to myself as I thought of a Jane Austin quote: *I have little pleasure in seeing my friends unless I'm fit to be seen.* When I was quite ready I was about to open the kitchen door and reveal myself in all my radiant glory when the door bell rang again.

Down I went to answer it again, and there stood my date. 'Oh Keith!' I stammered. 'I thought you were already here.'

'No,' he said. 'I've only just arrived. I'm not late am I?'

I smacked my hand to my mouth and exclaimed, 'Oh my God, who have I got in the kitchen?' I flew back up the stairs, pursued by Keith and sourly observed by Mrs. Moss, who'd emerged from her sitting-room to see what was going on, and flung open the kitchen door to find a bewildered looking former boyfriend sitting there. He explained he was on leave from the army (National Service) and had only called on the off-chance.

I stood for a few seconds staring stupidly from one to the other, until Keith said peevishly, 'Well, make up your mind, who are you going out with then.'

With apologies to Cyril, I decided to keep my date with Keith, and Cyril quietly went on his way. When Keith asked me where I'd like to go, I suggested a popular bar and restaurant in town known as The Gaity. (No... there were no such things as *gays* in those days, just good old-fashioned *queers)*.

As we entered I was marginally discomforted to see Cyril sitting alone at one of the dining tables. Starving hungry as I was by now, I presumed Keith would guide me to a table and ask the waiter for a menu. Not a bit of it. He strode straight up to the bar and brusquely asked, 'What will you have, draught or bottle?'

Cyril glanced at me, eyebrows arched quizzically. I'd never liked the taste of beer anyway, and I felt quite insulted to have been given such a mean choice, especially in front of someone whom I knew would have treated me better.

'Oh, neither, thank you,' I said, with a gracious smile, 'but would you excuse me a moment?' Then, with as much dignity as possible, I made my way to the door marked 'Ladies' and disappeared into the night.

When I got home I smiled ruefully to myself when I thought what a lot of trouble I'd gone to look my best, just to sit and eat a piece of cheese on toast on my own. Ah well - that's life!

Chapter 36

You Can Run.

It was while I was in my twenties that quite by chance I became an amateur athlete. Muriel had eventually followed in my footsteps and joined the WAAF, met a sailor and was shortly to get married. She came on leave to see me and on my day off on the Saturday, for something to, do we went to a local fete. Amongst the many attractions there were some sporting events, which included a hundred yards sprint for ladies, the prize for the winner being a set of saucepans.

'*You* can run, why don't you enter?' said Muriel, (who firmly believed I could do anything she set her mind to) then you can give me the saucepans for a wedding present.'

She got her saucepans, and it was the beginning of a new chapter in my life too. A man came up to me after the race and asked what athletic club I belonged to. I told him I didn't belong to any athletic club and asked him why he wanted to know. He said he was a coach at the Coventry Godiva's Athletic Club and invited me to their next training session for a trial. Much of my spare time over the next three years or more was spent being an amateur athlete. I was too late a starter to be brilliant, but I did have a measure of success, the highlight of my athletic achievement being selected to represent the Midlands at an athletic event at the White City Stadium, London, following the 1948 Olympics. I was pleased to have been chosen, but any illusions I might have cherished of becoming a really top athlete were quickly dispelled when I was soundly beaten by the likes of Dorothy Tyler, Dorothy Manley and the invincible Fanny Blankers-Kohen. However, during my time as an athlete with the Godiva Harriers, I did accumulate a number of watches, clocks, cutlery sets and powder compacts etcetera, which I eventually sold (although this was, at the time, strictly against the rules) and with the money I bought myself a 1936 Ford Eight car. A bit of an old banger admittedly, but I learned to drive and passed my test in it and I was more proud of that little old car than any vehicle I've owned since.

Chapter 37

Another Fine Mess

Sadly, the car met with an untimely end shortly after I passed my test, when it was being driven by Bill, the current boy friend. We'd travelled miles together in my beloved old banger, me as the learner and he in the passenger seat as the qualified driver, from where he offered advice and criticism and occasionally threw his hands over his face in alarm when I did the silly things that learners often do. It was during this time that he proposed. Not wishing to turn him down flat, not at least that is, until I'd passed my driving test, I said that I would *think about it.* It did not occur to me that this could be construed as a positive response, so I was a bit nonplussed when he turned up with an engagement ring on our next date.

We went out with a couple of friends the following evening to celebrate, but I felt so uncomfortable about the *celebration* that I developed a nervous headache and felt sick. So I asked Bill if he would drive me home. It was the first time he'd driven my car and I was not in the least impressed with his handling of it, but thought anyone who drove a motorbike and had piloted bomber planes during the war should know what he was doing, so I maintained a seething silence and suffered.

Then it happened. He failed to negotiate a bend, hit a bumpy roadside verge, over-corrected a few times, until the car finally came to a stop, upside down on the verge. I somehow got flung out of the backdoor, landing on my head with my feet in the air, whilst he crawled, unscathed out of the driving seat. My beloved little motor was deemed a "write-off", but the most shocking thing was when Bill said to me, 'If the police get involved we'd better say you were driving.'

'And why should I say that?' I demanded indignantly.

'Well, er...,' he said, stroking his chin, (he always did that when he was *thinking*).

'Well er... what!?' I said impatiently.

'Well, I haven't actually got a driving licence,' he confessed.

I was astonished and furious to think of all the miles we'd travelled together, with me thinking everything was legal and above board when in fact, he'd lied to me all this time. Luckily (for him) the police didn't get involved, but it gave me the excuse I'd been looking for. I tried to give him his ring back, but he insisted I keep it and if needs be, sell it and put the money towards another car. We remained friends and when I bought my next car – a 1939 Ford Eight this time – I said he could take his driving test in it. He did and he failed!

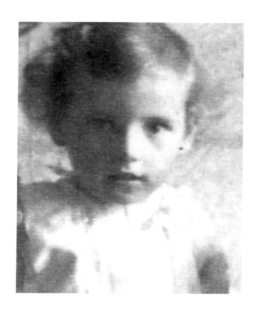

Only photograph of author as a child.

Author in centre – Valley Gardens Harrogate 1941

Sprinting Pots Coventry Godiva Harriers 1949

Author in her mid-thirties

Peggy looking pensive

Author on Meg

Lynn and Clare on Conroy and Meg

We sometimes went for a drive in the trap

Clare and Lynn entertaining Jonathan

Hard work has certainly paid off for Miss Lynne Trowbridge.

For she's earned herself the title of Branch Manager of the Year at John Blundell Limited, Windsor Street, Leamington, where she has worked for the last 18 years.

And to go with the title the firm, which has 150 branches in the country, presented her with a new Mini car last week.

Miss Trowbridge, who lives at 23 Newbold Terrace, Leamington, was promoted to branch manager a year ago — the first woman to hold the post in the firm.

The campaign to find the top branch manager was launched six months ago and points were awarded to each branch for their sales targets and promotions.

C/8/21/S

John Blundell's Branch Manager of the Year Award

Chapter 38

A Hairy Experience.

After I'd finished with the athletics I cast around for some other means of supplementing my income from my office job and started giving riding lessons in my spare time. I used to park my car in Seth the blacksmith's yard, where I also kept Dolly, my black pony. Besides being a farrier, Seth was also a horse dealer and there were always three or four horses about the place waiting for a buyer. Seth was old and a bit arthritic, but very brave on the ground with a whip in his hand, and I was the one who tried out any horses brought into the yard to be sold and give an opinion on them. Those horses I deemed suitable for such activity I would use to give riding lessons, or take riders on hacks before they were sold on, sharing the takings with Seth. But getting up on a strange horse about which one knew nothing except what the dealer chose to tell one, was sometimes a hazardous business and often fraught with danger. I had quite a few hairy experiences but one in particular sticks in my mind.

A dealer from Swindon turned up early one evening with four horses for sale. Two passed muster, one I rejected because it stumbled a lot and the other was a beautiful, 15.2 hands black gelding, with a white star and four white fetlocks. As it was beginning to get dark I said I would try this one out the following morning before going to work. The asking price was remarkably cheap for such a handsome horse with perfect conformation and a vet's certificate confirming he was sound in wind and limb. There had to be a catch somewhere.

At six-thirty the following morning I walked to the blacksmith's yard, thrilling, as I always did, at the solitary early morning sound of hammer striking anvil. The horse was already saddled and bridled, but as soon as Seth legged me up, I

128

knew I'd got a handful. We skittered wildly about the yard until I got him sufficiently under control to take him out onto the road, where, despite my efforts to keep him under control and show him who was boss, the second I eased my hands, he was off in a mad gallop. Up the road we flew until we reached a T junction, where I knew if I turned right and continued along this street we would be met by a steep grassy bank at the dead end of the road, which would surely bring us to a halt. It did, but only for a few brief seconds. Whilst I was trying to make up my mind whether to jump off and lead the horse back, or stay on board and ride it back, the horse had its own idea about what to do and up the bank it scrambled. I knew there was a path at the top which led to some fields and decided that when we reached them I would let him go and when he had enough and galloped himself out I would help him to a bit more. But in the scramble up the bank I lost a stirrup, the saddle slipped beneath the horse's belly and I found myself galloping along the narrow path, bare back with the saddle dangling uselessly beneath the horse's belly.

The path was narrow and men walking to work were having to back into the hedges so as not to get mown down. I had to do something drastic to avoid crashing into anyone who couldn't get out of the way in time, so I leapt off at full gallop, brought my left hand down over the horse's nostrils to restrict its breathing, and finally brought it under control, but not before, during the melee, it had lashed out with its back legs and caught me on my right ankle. I felt a thump but no pain. A man whom I'd nearly flattened in my wild escapade walked back towards me and I was sure he was going to tell me off. Ready to offer my apologies, he surprised me by congratulating me on my acrobatics and asked if I needed any help. I felt a bit of a fool but accepted his offer and asked him if he would go to the other side of the horse's head and help me lead it back to the stables. We got back without too much trouble, but it was only when I reached the safety of the blacksmith's yard that I experienced the most excruciating pain in my ankle and sank to the ground in agony. An X-ray revealed I'd crushed the bone.

Needless to say, we did not keep the horse, and I found out later from some gypsy dealers at Stow Fair that the horse was a '*wrong un*' known to be *yampee* and they averred that it would kill somebody one day. So *that* was why it was so cheap. I didn't know its ultimate fate, but I made sure the dealer knew how dangerous the animal was when he came to pick it up.

Chapter 39

Taxi Sir?

Sadly, after Seth died, the yard, stabling and blacksmith's shop, which were part of the adjacent old coaching inn were leased to a company of wrought iron workers and there was no more livery or horse-shoeing. So I had to find a new home for my little mare and think of another way of supplementing my office wages in my spare time, so that I could keep her fed and watered, and keep my old car going.

Not that I had that much time to spare for part-time work for in the summer I was playing team tennis, and in the winter league table tennis; but I was still young and fit and with energy to spare. So when a friend of mine who ran a taxi business asked me if I could do a bit of taxi driving for him, I readily agreed.

The year was 1960 and it was the lead up to Christmas, a time of year which, for varying reasons, I never really looked forward to. I didn't enjoy the boozy, exuberant excesses and the obligation to party and be jolly, and I never liked the shopping much either, always fretting that my gifts were unsuitable or not good enough. Then there was the ever pressing problem as to with whom I should spend Christmas. Living alone, as I happily did, there were many invitations from well-intentioned friends to join them, and, of course, there was always Muriel and her family, and I would invariably be thrown into agonies of indecision as to where I should be. And then, I seldom felt happy about where I was, for feeling guilty about where I was not. By agreeing to drive a taxi over the Christmas period, I had the perfect excuse for not going anywhere.

Streamline Taxis had a fleet of Austin Sixteen cars, none of which was totally reliable and would certainly not have passed muster with today's stringent safety regulations. They were noted for being heavy on the steering and had a back-end that would, under certain road conditions, swish about like a demented snake. But I was undaunted and notwithstanding the bad road conditions, I really enjoyed the first few hours of duty, mostly ferrying men from one pub to another and being rewarded handsomely for my trouble with large tips.

All was going well until I was asked to pick up a fare take him to Stoneleigh, but then discovered I had a flat tyre.

'Take this other car,' said Wally, the proprietor. 'It's got a bit of a dodgy clutch but you should be okay. I'll have the tyre fixed by the time you get back.'

Off I went to pick up my fare, who turned out to be a gentleman with a thick Irish brogue, his speech being made the more unintelligible by the fact that he'd obviously had a lot to drink. He stumbled into the back seat of the taxi and when I asked him to confirm his destination, through his be-fuddled slur he mumbled, 'Stoneleigh.'

This was a small village about six miles away, so small in fact that it didn't even have a pub or a church. Given his state of inebriation, I was concerned that he might throw up in the taxi, but I needn't have worried. Shortly into the journey he must have fallen asleep for he began snoring very loudly.

The foggy drizzle was now beginning to freeze, making the roads icy and I knew it would probably get worse. The approach road to the village was down a long steep hill with a sharp left turn at the bottom over a river bridge and I was anxious lest the car should slide out of control. It was a relief when we arrived safely in the village and I roused my slumbering passenger to ask him where, in Stoneleigh he wanted to be.

'Shstoneligh, Shstoneleigh,' was the only positive thing I could pick out from his befuddled ramblings. 'Well you're in

Stoneleigh,' I said testily, 'so would you get out of the cab please Sir.'

With some help from me he struggled out of the cab and staggered around looking confused and disoriented. He paid me the exact fare with no tip and I left him to decide where he lived and began my journey back. The weather was worsening and I soon realised, as I got part of the way up the steep, icy incline, that I was going nowhere. Despite maximum revs and much waggling of the steering wheel, the car refused to go any further forward and gradually began sliding back down the hill. Given the instability of the road holding capabilities of the car at the best of times, the now total clutch failure and the increasingly poor visibility, I cautiously steered the car backwards onto the grass verge. No such refinements as 'in-car' telephones or mobiles in those days and as far as I knew, no bus service on Christmas Day either, so I found myself stuck in the middle of nowhere, without a house or telephone box in sight. Nothing for it but to walk back to Leamington and hope a passing car might give me a lift. But no car came and I had to walk all the way.

When, worried and weary, I eventually arrived at the taxi office, Wally greeted me with a mixture of relief and annoyance.

'Where have you been?' he demanded, 'and what took you so long?'

After explaining what had happened, he stared at me incredulously, then said, 'But what were you doing in Stoneleigh?'

'I took my last fare there,' I said.

'Oh my God!' he exclaimed. 'Where is he now?'

'Still there I presume,' I shrugged. 'But why are you so bothered about *him*?'

'Because,' he said, 'he only wanted to go to the Stoneleigh Pub, which is just up the road from here.'

I still wonder, to this day, what happened to that poor, drunken Irishman wandering around in the cold and dark in a remote, isolated village in the middle of nowhere.

Chapter 40

Shattered Illusions.

Life in my thirties was good. I'd made a lot of progress in my job, had a good social life and still indulged in a variety of sporting activities. Muriel now had two children - Christopher nine and Susan four and her husband had been promoted to a petty officer and was serving on the Royal Yacht Britannia. She had a nice council house in Minster-on-Sea, Kent, and I felt I could, finally, relax the responsibility I'd always felt for her happiness and well being.

I arranged to spend a week's holiday with them at the same time that Gordon was on leave, so that he could practise driving my car every day hoping it would help him pass his driving test which had been booked for the end of the week.

All seemed to be going well, except that Gordon seemed bad tempered and irritable towards the end of his leave and I put it down to the fact that, despite my best efforts to help him - he failed his driving test. It wasn't until the last morning of the holiday that I became aware that there was a real problem. I was in the kitchen making an early morning cup of tea when four year old Susan came running down the stairs and flew into the kitchen.

'Aunty Lynn! Aunty Lynn!' she said urgently. 'My Daddy's leaving us today.'

'Of course he is, darling,' I said. 'His leave is up and he has to go back to his ship.'

'No. No!' she insisted. 'He's leaving us for good. I heard him telling Mummy.'

Muriel appeared in the kitchen shortly after. 'Are you all right Muriel?' I asked, as I watched her struggle to keep her composure.

'Yes. We're all right,' she said.

It wasn't until I questioned her further that she burdened me with the truth. When I asked how long she'd known, she said he'd told her at the beginning of his leave but she'd hoped he would change his mind.

To say I was shocked and furious was an understatement, not only because he was breaking up the marriage to go off with another woman (which was really nothing to do with me) but to think how he'd manipulated and used me to suit his own selfish ends.

I asked Muriel why she hadn't told me when I first arrived and was very touched when she said, 'Christopher begged me not to tell you as he didn't want to spoil your holiday.'

Gordon went back from his leave and never saw his family again or kept in contact with them, but we learned through various sources that he eventually married the woman he'd left her for. They eventually divorced and he married twice more after that.

I felt that old responsibility for her welfare returning, a responsibility which I'd managed to partially shed over the years, but now, it was not only for her I felt a duty towards, but her children also. So I made the three hundred and fifty miles round trip down to Kent and back at week-ends as often as I could to try and brighten up their lives a bit and help ease the financial burden of their reduced circumstances. But all this travelling meant I no longer had time or energy for part-time jobs to supplement my income. So I sold my horse and although I was happy in my job, after fifteen years with the same company, I decided to look for another position where I would have the possibility of earning more money.

Chapter 41

Pastures New.

It wasn't long before a friend told me there was a vacancy for a Sales Rep at the firm where he worked, so I went along for an interview, without much hope of landing the job as the firm was mostly male oriented and if I were to be successful, I would be the only lady rep working at the Leamington Branch of John Blundell Ltd. It doesn't sound much now, but the basic wage was a £1 a week more than I was already earning, with the opportunity of boosting my wages with commission on sales. A vehicle was also provided, so it seemed it might be a good move, although I'd never had any experience of selling. Lack of experience and the fact that I was a woman notwithstanding, I was offered the job and after a lot of soul searching decided to take it.

I was in for a bit of a culture shock at first. The job was tough and I was having to deal with all manner of people, but having relinquished my nice, safe, cushy job as office manager I'd now burnt my boats and could not afford to look back or have any regrets; so I just got on with it and gave the job my best shot. I've never had much of a sense of direction and still haven't, so having to call on at least thirty customers a day was not easy and I frequently would not finish work before seven or eight o'clock at night and then have my paperwork to do before I could call it a day. Most of the goods sold, which ranged from furniture, electrical appliances, carpets, clothing and anything in between, were obtained on credit or hire purchase and the money was collected on a weekly basis, the idea being that as the debt diminished, it was kept open with further sales. This worked very well, but the hardest part of the job I found, was having the courage and common sense to refuse further credit if the customers were struggling to pay off the money they already owed.

It was so easy to rub one's hands with glee when someone wanted to order a large item of furniture, carpet or whatever, only to wring them in anguish later, when it transpired that the customer had not the will or ability to maintain their regular weekly payments, thereby creating toxic debt and disaster. But no matter how careful one tried to be, there were rare occasions when even I would be conned. I remember one particular customer whom I thought I knew reasonably well. He ordered a lot of new furniture, and as a precaution I asked him for a much larger deposit than was normal and advised him how much his weekly payments would be.

'No problem at all,' he assured me, as he pulled out a roll of notes and handed me the money I'd asked for. I spoke with his wife who was all smiles and friendliness and she also assured me the repayments would be no problem. The goods were duly delivered and I was pleased, thinking of all the commission I'd earned. Pleased that is, until I went to the house the following week to find they'd done a moonlight flit. The house was empty and no one knew where they'd gone.

Then there was the customer who won over £350,000 on the football pools, which was an absolute fortune in those days. They cleared their outstanding debt with us, moved from their council house in Leamington, bought a large farmhouse in the country and populated the pasture land with thoroughbred horses, which neither she nor her husband could ride nor had any idea how to look after. They also had an indoor swimming pool built, bought expensive cars, had wild parties and generally lived it up. Within less than five years, they were bankrupt; the husband died of a heart attack and the wife was living back in a council flat. I felt sorry for her when she contacted me to see if I could let her have a small rug to put on the bare boards of her bedroom. She echoed my thoughts when she ruefully commented: 'From rags to riches back to rags. Who'd have thought it eh?'

Sometimes the branch manager would come on my round with me, ostensibly to check my ledgers, but we always ended up having lunch at The Roebuck Inn in Warwick. One day we knocked on the door of a middle-aged, orange-haired customer at my usual time of about 9.30 in the morning. Expecting it would be me, the lady answered the door in a low-cut, see-through nylon nightdress.

'Oh, sorry, hang on a minute,' she said, quickly closing the door when she saw a man standing beside me. Shortly, the door opened again and the large, pendulously bosomed lady re-appeared, still in her see-through nightdress. 'Sorry to keep you waiting,' she said, 'I hadn't got me teeth in.'

Another of my more memorable customers was a delightful Welsh lady who was a Friday evening call. She lived at the top of a block of flats in Warwick and by the time I'd panted up the several flights of stairs I was glad of a sit down and a short chat. She always had a bottle of sherry on a small table beside her chair and never failed to try and induce me to take a glass with her, which, of course, I had to refuse. But I liked her and didn't mind having a brief chat now and again.

'How are you today Carwen?' I enquired, after I'd completed our business.

'I'm fed-up. I'm bloody fed-up,' she said.

'Oh dear, what's made you so fed up?'

'Well – it's 'im, isn't it. He goes out every Friday night and always comes home drunk and he do drive me bloody mad. I wouldn't mind if he sat down quiet like or went to bed, but he do always sing and then he do say, "Clap, you dull bugger, clap!" and I do have to clap him. Well, I wouldn't care,' she continued, 'but he do always sing the same thing: *When you do walk through a bloody storm.*'

She poured herself another sherry, then, raising her glass, smiled artfully and said, 'I do have to have my sherry to help me put up with the drunken bastard.'

Chapter 42

Another Challenge

It used to be said, with some justification, that if a woman wanted to progress in a male dominated workplace, she had to be twice as good as any man. I'm not sure whether I was twice as good as a man, but I always met and frequently surpassed my sales targets, and although more women were now being employed by the company as sales reps, mostly very successfully, we knew our place and accepted it.

So I was a bit surprised when I called to Head Office in London to be interviewed for promotion to branch supervisor, especially as no other woman in the company held this position. The incentives on offer made it seem worthwhile so I accepted the challenge and did my best to prove the company's faith in my ability was not misplaced. I was a good motivator and knew how to get the best out of the team for which I was responsible, so that our results always met and often surpassed the set targets. After I'd been doing a supervisor's job for a few years our branch manager was promoted and moved on and I was offered his job.

Since I was now the first and only woman to be made a manager, I worked harder than ever to expand the business. Because of this I needed more staff and when I advertised the vacancies I said I would be conducting interviews from ten o'clock on a certain morning. I went to the office where I planned to do the interviewing and was alarmed to see a queue of about twenty people of both sexes and all ages waiting to see me, and I spent a lot of time which I could ill afford interviewing them all. One lady who'd joined the queue was duly ushered into my presence. She looked rather elderly and seemed not at all sure of herself and I made up my mind at once that she would not be suitable, but thought it only polite to go through the motions anyway.

'What is your name?'

'And address?

'Date of Birth?'

'Your present and past work experience?'

'Do you hold a current driving licence?

When the answer to the last question was 'No' I seized the moment and was about to say, 'I'm awfully sorry but...' when she interrupted me.

'Excuse me,' she said, ' why do you want to know all these things?

'It's standard procedure when applying for a job,' I said.

'But I've only come in to buy a pair of shoes,' she exclaimed indignantly.

The next time I advertised a job, I dictated the advertisement to one of the office staff to put into the local paper, part of which should have read: "Active, outgoing person invited to apply, in writing, for the following position..."

I was puzzled when I had several replies, each one extravagantly extolling their physical attributes, some even giving their bust sizes. It wasn't until I read the newspaper advertisement that I realised my instruction had been misheard and instead of '*Active* outgoing person' it had been printed as '*Attractive* outgoing person.'

Not long after I took over the Branch it was decided by Head Office that they would run a competition over a period of six months to find the top manager in the country, the first prize for which would be a Mini car. There were incentives for all the staff too and there was great excitement when, after the six month period was up, the final results were announced and I was adjudged the top manager.

The firm's annual conference was to be held at our London Headquarters   shortly after the results were known, and I, together with the hundred and fifty other branch managers in the company was required to attend, and on which occasion I would be ceremoniously handed the keys of the car I had won.

On previous visits to Head Office I had travelled by car, but on this occasion, of course, I had to take the train so that I could drive the prize car home.

It was a warm, sunny summer day when I set out on my journey from Leamington, and I was bubbling with eager anticipation at the thought of the day that lay before me. I'd had my hair done the day before, and had taken great care in applying my make-up before starting off on my journey in order to present myself to the best advantage. I'd also bought some new clothes for the occasion: a cream coloured pure silk blouse, a fashionable, figure hugging skirt and high heeled light brown shoes with handbag to match. So pleased was I with my appearance that when I got to Paddington I popped into a photo booth to photograph myself, as a future reminder of how good I thought I looked for this special occasion.

The line of taxis I'd seen waiting at the station when I got off the train had now mysteriously disappeared and I had to wait for one to return. There were a few other people waiting but although I was at the front of the queue, when a taxi pulled up I was rudely elbowed out of the way by some foreign lady who was obviously in a great hurry to get to Victoria Station. I approached the next taxi to arrive but when I told him my destination he inexplicably told me to get the next taxi, which came soon after. This taxi didn't seem keen on having me as a fare either, but by now I was becoming very anxious, so after a bit of pleading, he grudgingly agreed to take me. We started off and he asked my destination again. 'John Blundells, Sommerford Grove, Stoke Newington,' I repeated.

He then surprised me by asking if I knew the way. Of course I don't know the bloody way I thought, but meekly replied, 'I'm sorry, I'm a complete stranger round here.'

143

He then began to consult his map whilst we were on the move, which I thought a bit dangerous given the volume of traffic. Besides, I thought taxi drivers were supposed to know their way everywhere.

It was a relief when he said, 'I've got it,' as he tossed his map back onto the passenger seat beside him. We slowly ground our way through the heavy traffic as the minutes swiftly moved on towards the time of the meeting..

At last he pulled up and said, 'This is it.'

I looked about me and nothing I saw looked anything like "It". I'd visited Head Office previously so had some idea of what the building looked like and its immediate surroundings.

'No, No,' I protested. 'This isn't where I want to be at all.'

'You said you wanted Sommerford Grove and this is it,' he said, pointing to a sign on the wall that clearly confirmed his statement.

'Well will you drive to the other end,' I pleaded, 'because I know this isn't where I want to be.'

'No,' he said. 'There's no right turn and I haven't got time to make a detour.' Bewildered, I paid him off then took stock of my bearings. Nothing looked familiar, but I walked to the other end of Sommerford Grove and, as I suspected, the premises I was looking for were nowhere to be seen. The weather, which had been so pleasant when I started my journey, had now been replaced by blustery showers and I had no coat. I saw a dustcart and asked the driver if he could help. 'Go back along the way you've come,' he said, "turn right onto the main road and it's about a hundred yards down on your left.'

I hastily re-traced my steps, (or as hastily as I could that is, for by now my feet were killing me) following the instructions I'd been given to the letter, but still couldn't find the building I was looking for. I made my way back to where I'd been dropped off by the taxi, in the vain hope that somehow John Blundells Head Office would miraculously appear before my eyes. Of course it didn't, and by now I was tired, soaking wet, thoroughly dishevelled, and wandering about as if in a daytime nightmare that had no end.

It was now past the time I should have been at the meeting and I asked someone if they could direct me to the nearest telephone kiosk.

'Where are you?' asked the voice at the other end.

'I wish I knew,' I said desperately. 'Oh, hang on,' I added, as I popped my head outside to ask a passing pedestrian.

'Tottenham Court Road..'

'Tottenham Court Road,' I repeated into the mouthpiece.

'Oh my God,' said the voice. 'They've dropped you off at the wrong Sommerford Grove. Stay where you are. We'll send a car to pick you up.'

The Managing Director was none to pleased as I'd held up the meeting. And instead of arriving all glory, glamour and gracious smiles, the only woman in a sea of men, I slunk shame facedly into the conference room and tried to make myself invisible by squirming low in a seat at the back. My mind was in a turmoil and I looked thoroughly dishevelled with my hair wet and all awry, my tight skirt wetly hugging my backside and my soaked silk blouse clinging embarrassingly to my bosom. I was glad when it was the lunch break so that I could sidle off to the lady's toilet, repair my appearance and regain a measure of my usual composure.

The afternoon went well enough. I was given due honour for my achievement, the keys of the car were ceremoniously handed over to me and I was driven to the garage to take possession of my prize.

Possession was brief. Whilst waiting for the paper work to be completed, I wondered what I was going to do with two cars, already having a company car, and concluded I would have to sell it. So instead of driving it away, which would have made it immediately second-hand, I negotiated a fair deal with the garage and took the money instead.

It was when I was on the train homeward bound, thinking about the minor disasters and small triumphs of the day, that my thoughts took a backward somersault to my less than idyllic childhood, and I could perhaps be forgiven for thinking that I hadn't done so badly for myself after all.

The company ran the same type of competition twice more. I was only second the next time but won it again the third time, for each of which efforts I received fulsome recognition and handsome monetary rewards. Aside from helping Muriel with a bit of financial support, I also bought a caravan with some of the money and kept it on the land of a farmer friend.

I'd had enough of living under the ever watchful eye and trivial, carping complaints of Mrs. Moss, so at last, I moved and went to live in the caravan at the farm until such time the farm cottage was decorated and fit for me to move into. This was when I first met Joe, who, with his brother, was doing some work on the cottage. I learned he was divorced but kept custody of his little boy – Lloyd – who was now about five or six and was being looked after by his sister-in-law. I had no romantic interest in Joe, but he became a good friend and was easy company, and although he didn't know it – after getting to know him a bit better - I had designs on him.

I was still visiting Muriel and her family in Kent about once a month, hoping my visits might help to cheer their lives. But it was a long and irksome journey, and I sometimes wished to be spared it. On one of my proposed visits I asked Joe if he would like to come with me for the ride. The poor, unsuspecting chap readily agreed and always accompanied me thereafter. It wasn't long before I suggested that I would look after the kids if he and Muriel would like to go out for the evening.

My plans came to fruition and eventually Joe got a job in Kent, moved there with Lloyd, his little boy; he and Muriel got married and I was quite happy for her to believe that she had 'pinched' him off me.

Chapter 43

The Visit.

It was after the incident with the waitress at the Saxon Mill Hotel, when I was asked if I was one of the *Home Girls* that I began to think again about my early beginnings, and the urge came to visit the little valley where I was born and spent the early years of my life. So the next time I was due for a week's holiday I spent the first few days organising the move from my caravan into the farm cottage (which was now ready to be occupied) and arranging the sale of the caravan. This accomplished, I decided to make the visit, even if it was only to stand and remember...

I had little expectation that there would be anyone in the village who would remember me or even wish to see me, but the one person I remembered more vividly than any other was Mrs. Coles, who had been so kind to us as children. I found the street where we had lived and gazed long and hard at the house we had occupied, but felt too shy to knock on the door. Then I took my courage in my hands and knocked on the door of the house where I knew Mrs. Coles had lived.

It was opened by the very person I was hoping to see. She looked almost exactly as I'd remembered her all those years ago. Plain, though kindly features, ruddy complexion, hair short and straight and parted to one side, held in place with wire grips. She was wearing the same type of apron she'd always worn – a sleeveless wrap-over secured with a tie-string.

'Mrs. Coles?' I said, raising my eyebrows.

'Yes,' she replied, looking puzzled. 'I don't *know* you, do I?'

'Well you do, actually,' I said, 'but you probably don't remember me.'

I was about to introduce myself when another person appeared in the doorway, whom I took to be her daughter – Mary – who had been one of my erstwhile friends.

'O Mamma, Mamma, you know who it is don't you. It's Lynn Trowbridge as was,' she cried excitedly.

Mrs. Coles' jaw fell open in surprise and she reeled backwards, then quickly recovered herself, opened her arms wide in welcome and said, 'Oh come you in. Come you in now and sit yourself down.'

I sat myself down on the highly polished wooden armchair indicated and accepted her offer of a cup of tea.

'Where have you come from?' she asked as she poured the tea. I told her.

'Well, well, after all these years,' she breathed. 'It's so lovely to see you. I can't believe it! You've driven a long way then haven't you. Now, you are going to stop the night aren't you?'

It was a statement rather than a question, but much as I would have liked to stay the night, I declined her offer, explaining that I had to get back as I was moving into a cottage the next day and someone was coming in the morning to buy my caravan.

Ever ready to be impressed (as Welsh people often are) she looked at me with undisguised admiration and exclaimed: 'You have a *cottage,* and a *caravan,* and a *car*, and you do talk like a nob don't you. Well, I suppose you *are* a nob really.'

She glanced at my ring-less left hand. 'You not married then?'

'No,' I replied, 'I'm not married.'

'Pity – nobody take to you? I see you've still got your own teeth.'

'Oh yes,' I said, widening my smile to prove it.

There was a boy of about twelve in the background who was introduced to me as Bryn, the son of Mary, but there was no mention of a husband.

'Bryn, go you now and fetch *yew-er* Uncle 'Endry,' Mrs. Coles commanded him.

Off he went and re-appeared with Uncle Endry.

'Now you know who this don't you?' said Mrs. Coles.

'No, I don't think so.' He shook his head looking puzzled.

'Well, it's Lynn Trowbridge as was – you remember her don't you?'

He thrust out his hand in genuine surprise and pleasure and exclaimed, 'Well I never! There's lovely to see you.'

'Now you're going to have something to eat aren't you?' entreated Mrs. Coles.

I said, 'If you have any of that cake you used to make every week I'd love a slice of that.'

She dabbed at the tears that sprung to her eyes as she went to the kitchen and emerged shortly after bearing a pot of tea and the very same cake, and indeed, it tasted the same as I remembered and I ate it with the same relish.

I began to feel a little bit tearful myself, but quickly pulled myself together when Mrs. Coles proudly related to Endry, 'She has a *cottage* and a *caravan* and a *car* and her own *teeth*, but not married mind.'

Uncle Endry raised his eyes and opened his mouth to show he was suitably impressed, then shifted awkwardly from one foot to the other and I wondered if he was remembering the time he last saw me, as a little girl, when I fled from the woods, terrified, because he'd tried to put his hand up my knickers.

Mrs. Coles turned to Bryn again. 'Go you now and fetch Mrs. Howells.'

Same routine: 'Now you know who this is don't you?'

'No, I don't think so.'

'Well, it's Lynn Trowbridge as was. You remember her don't you?'

Mrs. Coles proudly launched into her spiel once more. 'She has a cottage, and a caravan, and a car, and her own teeth. Not married mind.'

'Well I never,' said Mrs. Howells, then peered at me long and hard before remarking wonderingly, 'Well - you were such a *pretty* baby.'

During my short visit, it seemed half the village had been invited into Mrs. Coles' front room to come and marvel at this apparition from the past, who had all these material attributes, plus her own teeth and talked like a nob - but not married mind.

I loved the visit and when it was time to leave I was feeling quite euphoric, like some minor celebrity on a glory trip.

It was only when I was driving home that reality re-established itself and I smiled to myself as I reflected that my teeth were the only things I really *did* own: I was selling the caravan, renting the cottage and it was a company car.

I made another visit shortly after, but this time it was previously arranged and I took Muriel with me. Mrs. Coles gave us a rapturous welcome and had laid up the table for afternoon tea, with a white damask tablecloth, her best EPNS cutlery and her real china tea set. I remarked on the beautiful china and she replied, 'I only get it out for *funderals* and special occasions. I do call it my *funderal* tea set.'

As well as the daintily cut sandwiches, she also produced, yet again, the much loved fruit cake of yesteryear, and before we said our fond 'goodbyes' she gave me a tin with a whole cake in it to take home.

After taking our leave we went to visit our mother's grave. We had no idea where our father was buried but I remembered Mam was in the graveyard of a little church on the side of a windswept hill in Bedwas. As expected, there was no headstone to mark the spot, so we found the vicar who delved into the records, found the plan and told us where the plot was.

'Eighth along, third row down on your left, second plot.'

We followed his instructions and found a barely discernable mound in a row of other unmarked graves - and stood silently remembering. We gathered some wild flowers: buttercups, daisies, St. Anne's lace and red campion and reverently laid them on the mound. 'These are for you Mum,' I said.

The poignancy of the moment hit a tender spot and we turned away from each other to hide the tears of belated sorrow.

'God bless you Mum,' I mumbled, before making our way back to the car. It was a pilgrimage I was glad we made, but we never spoke of it again.

.

Chapter 44

Christmas at Middle Farm Cottage

Having moved from bed-sit to caravan to three bed room farm cottage, I was now able to invite Muriel, Joe and the family to stay with me for Christmas. Not since a very small child had I entered enthusiastically into the spirit of Christmas, but this year was different. So much so, that for the first time I put up decorations. Bits of holly and mistletoe festooned the oak beams, and a small, bauble be-decked, fairy-lighted Christmas Tree stood twinkling happily in a corner. Having no central heating, I'd lit coal fires in the sitting room and dining room and felt a glow of satisfaction as I watched the fires dart their flames of warmth and welcome.

Muriel, Joe and the three children, Chris twelve, Susan six, (from Muriel's first marriage) and Lloyd six, (from Joe's first marriage) arrived safely after a long journey from their home in Kent

After the children had gone to bed I took pleasure in helping fill their stockings with the traditional Christmas goodies of long ago – apple, orange, nuts, chocolate and a few stocking filler presents. Then we sat sipping sherry, oozing goodwill, and listening to Christmas music, and I went to bed happy, smugly thinking what a wonderful Christmas this was promising to be.

The following morning, after the unwrapping of presents, cries of feigned delight and general excitement, it was time to think of more practical things like the preparation of Christmas dinner. I'd won a large turkey in a raffle but I'd never cooked a turkey before and didn't like the look of it at all. Muriel hadn't cooked one either and we both felt squeamish about removing its long neck with the revolting red comb and impudent beak dangling on the end, so we asked Joe to do the necessary.

Deed done, turkey stuffed and all neatly wrapped in tin foil, Joe proudly conveyed the bird to the oven. It wouldn't fit!

'Oh my giddy aunt,' I exclaimed.

'Quite!' said nephew Chris.

'Oh no!' cried Muriel.

'Bleeding 'ell,' said Joe.

We were resigned to having a meatless Christmas dinner when Marjory Phillips – the farmer's wife – came over to wish us a Happy Christmas and bring some mince pies. She stayed chatting and we told her of our problem.

'Don't worry,' she said. 'I'll cook it in my oven, but it will have to wait until our turkey's finished cooking, if you don't mind.'

'Of course we don't mind,' I said, bursting with gratitude.

To while away the wait we all went for a walk. We marvelled at the abundance of red berries on the bushes; got sentimental at the sight of a robin and whooped with delight when we saw a few flurries of snow wafting about in the wayward wind.

When we got back there was great joy when Martin Phillips appeared with the turkey and we were finally able to sit down to our belated Christmas dinner. It was the first time I'd had the opportunity of having Muriel and her family to stay with me and this was going to be a real, old fashioned family Christmas.

Joe carved the turkey and I was not going to allow the fact that the meat looked pink instead of white to mar the feast, and covered the slightly under-cooked meat with gravy so it wouldn't be so noticeable. When everyone had been served, I even went so far as to suggest we said grace before we began to eat, and was in such good humour that I smiled, instead of scolding, when the children mischievously said, 'Grace.' Muriel thought it proper not to show that she thought it funny and Joe raised his eyes to the heavens and said, 'Kids eh?'

No one was able to do full justice to the main course, (which was disappointing after all the effort that had gone into preparing it) stating that they wanted to leave room for the pudding. I went to the kitchen and secretly inserted silver sixpenny pieces in it, heavily doused it in brandy, set it alight, then proudly bore it to the table, nicely enveloped in blue flame. We all had a helping, but I forgot to mention the sixpenny pieces until an anguished cry went up from Muriel.

'Oh no!' she wailed. 'I've chipped a tooth!'

'Oh bleeding 'ell,' said Joe.

Six year old Susan began to cough ominously. Not to be outdone, she said, 'I think I've swallowed mine.'

'Bleeding 'ell,' said Joe again, as Muriel leapt up to thump her on the back, whilst I searched frantically in her pudding to see if there was still a sixpence in it. There was!

'I haven't got a sixpence,' wailed Lloyd, so I gave him another helping of pudding and slyly stuck a sixpence in it. He ate all his pudding and still vowed he hadn't found a sixpence, at which point I was too tired to care whether he'd swallowed it or not.

The rest of the day passed in a blur of washing up, tidying up, making drinks, eating mince pies, and keeping the coal fires burning, until it was time to sink, exhausted, into bed. There was great excitement when we woke the next morning to find the world covered in a thick blanket of snow. Muriel, Lloyd and Joe went to visit his parents who lived about twelve miles away, whilst twelve year old Chris and sister Sue elected to stay with me.

Chris, at the time, was very much into Greek mythology and any subject that engaged his interest he would do to death, and do us to death telling us about it. What he had to say was interesting, but we could only take so much, so I suggested that he limited his talk to half an hour a day, when we could give him our full and undivided attention. I gave him his half hour, then busied myself in the kitchen. Shortly, Susan came running into the kitchen in a state of agitation. 'Aunty Lynn, Chrissie's doing it again. He's doing it again!'

'Oh God spare us!' I mumbled. 'What's he up to?'

'He's *doing it* again,' she said.

I charged into the living room, Susan hot on my heels, to find Chris looking a picture of innocence and mildly surprised. 'What are you doing Chris?' I demanded.

'Nothing,' he said.

'If you're doing nothing now, what *have* you been doing?' I demanded.

'Susan! What's he been doing?'

'Talking about Greek mythology again Aunty Lynn.'

'Well stop!' I said severely, trying to suppress a smile of relief.

We went outside and threw snowballs at each other, then built an imposing snowman.

Susan wanted to give him a name and after some discussion Chris said, 'Why can't it be a snowwoman, then we could call her Khione.'

'Khione,' I said. 'Where does that name come from?'

'She was the Greek goddess of snow and northerly winds.'

'Of course, how could I have forgotten?' I lied.

We bowed extravagantly and paid her mock homage before going back indoors, where they argued their way through a game of snakes and ladders whilst I made sandwiches with the slightly pink turkey which no one wanted, so we threw the rest out for the birds and gorged ourselves on chocolates and nuts instead.

The return in the early evening of Muriel, Joe and Lloyd from their visit to the in-laws was heralded by an alarming thud. I went outside to investigate, only to discover that it was freezing hard on top of the snow and although Joe had safely negotiated the long drive down the lane to the farm, when he applied his brakes to stop, his car had skidded into mine.

'Oh no,' cried Muriel, as we surveyed the damage to their car.

'Bleeding 'ell!' said Joe.

'Not to worry,' I said. 'The bit of damage to my car will be fixed by the firm, and there's not much damage to yours either. Let's forget it and go in and make a cup of tea.'

We hurried into the house out of the freezing cold and I went to the kitchen to put the kettle on. No water came. I tried the bathroom. No water.

'Joe!' I called from the kitchen. 'There's no water coming out of the taps.'

'Bleeding 'ell,' he said. 'The pipes must be frozen.'

'Oh no!' wailed Muriel.

Joe went to the farm to see if they had any water. They had, so Mr. Phillips and his son brought buckets of hot water over to unfreeze the lead piping. They applied towels soaked in the hot water and there was great rejoicing when the water in the kitchen began to flow once more. I filled the kettle and plugged it in, made my way back to the living room and was horrified to see the tiled hallway swimming in water. The pipes that had been frozen had swollen and split. More frantic activity: me mopping up the floor, Joe and the Phillips family trying to bind the pipes, Muriel standing around looking aghast and the kids thoroughly enjoying the drama of it all. Muriel ordered them to go to the lavatory before the pipes froze again, the last one only – to pull the chain.

Once things were more-or-less under control, I went back to the kitchen to make the long promised cup of tea. The kettle had disappeared, with only the cord hanging forlornly from its socket.

'What's happened to the kettle,' I demanded.

A quick search revealed it lurking in the opposite corner of the kitchen. In all the excitement, I'd forgotten I'd put it on. No automatic switch-off in those days. The kettle had boiled dry and forcefully self-ejected.

I swore like the proverbial fish wife and Muriel said my language was reprehensible, to which I retorted, 'I don't bloody care. *I've had e-bloody- nough'*

After getting the kids off to bed, we sat in the companionable warmth and glow of the coal fire, sipping wine and laughing like fools at all the things that had gone wrong that evening, whilst Muriel, between giggles, kept saying, 'That's typical of you.'

I wasn't sure which part was *typical of me*. It wasn't my fault the turkey was too big for the oven; nor that it was marginally under-cooked. Perhaps it *was* my fault that I hadn't warned them about the sixpences in the plum pudding, causing her tooth to break, but it wasn't *me* who'd skidded into my car. It wasn't my fault either that there was no central heating in the cottage, causing the lead pipes to freeze then burst, and I certainly couldn't be held responsible for the weather. But Muriel always liked someone to be accountable, and as it was my home, I suppose it was only right that it should be me. However, we continued to laugh and see the funny side of everything and finally went to bed, Muriel happy and confirmed in her belief that I wasn't quite *normal.*

I remember once saying to her: 'Well, Muriel, if I'm as witless as you seem to believe I am, how do you think I've held down the responsible job I have all these years?'

'We've often wondered,' she said.

I got up early the next morning, lit the fires, made a fry-up breakfast and boiled the water in a saucepan to make the tea. Over breakfast, the disasters of the day before weren't mentioned and when it was time for them to leave it was all smiles and hugs and hearty thanks and protestations that despite the problems they'd really enjoyed themselves.

After they'd gone, I went round to the back garden, looked at Goddess Khione, standing proud in all her frozen glory, then bowed and said, 'Thank you. Despite all, that *was* one of the best Christmases I can remember.'

Chapter 45

It Takes all Sorts.

I must have been in my late thirties when I met John. Although I'd had three engagements and several boy friends in the past, I knew I wasn't marriageable material. I just couldn't bring myself to share a bed with a man or commit to an exclusive relationship. But John was different. He was good looking, good fun, a good dancer, and openly *gay*. He thought I might be too, and although I protested that I wasn't, I did sometimes wonder, when I remembered the brief affair with my first love – Denise – and how my WAAF friend Molly and I had been romantically attracted to each other, even if we never spoke of it.

My curiosity got the better of me when John suggested we visit a gay pub in Walsall that he knew and I agreed to go along, more as an interested observer than anything.

'Hello darling,' said a theatrical, heavily made up lady to John as we walked in, 'and who is your lovely friend?'

John introduced us. 'This is Lynn - Lynn, this is Noshka.'

'How d'you do,' I said politely. Then thought: Wouldn't you know, someone looking like a carbon copy of *Carmen Miranda* would have to have an exotic name like Noshka.

'What would you like to drink, darling?' she gushed embarrassingly.

I would have preferred not to have been asked by this person, but John came to the rescue and saved my blushes by saying, 'No Noshka, I'll get this round.'

Then I noticed a man sitting at the bar staring in our direction. Sleazy looking creep, I thought, why does he keep staring over here. Shortly, he left his perch and drifted over to join us, offering to buy me another drink, but I was able to politely refuse, explaining I had to be careful as I was driving.

Noshka introduced him as her husband – Peter. I smiled and exchanged a few pleasantries, then he asked me if I knew the group of women who were standing opposite. I glanced across and said that I didn't, but why did he ask.

'Oh, I just wondered,' he said, with an enigmatic smile.

I chanced another look, this time with more interest, to observe a group of women who were laughing and chatting and who were, quite obviously, what they were. These are *real* lesbians (hate the word) I thought. I'd never knowingly met a group of women like this before and I was intrigued. One stood out from the others because she was taller, better looking and had a pleasant smile, with which I was favoured every time she glanced in my direction.

After a while I began to feel that this wasn't a place I really wanted to be and suggested to John that we should move on.

'Don't go darling,' pleaded Noshka. 'Why don't you both come back to our place. We'll have a party. Is there anyone here you'd like me to invite?'

Before answering I looked at John who was all for it, then glanced across the room at the group of women who'd held my interest earlier. The tall one smiled and winked and I was mildly intrigued, so with a modicum of misgiving I said to Noshka, 'Yes, that would great. Are you going to ask those ladies over there?'

The booze was bought and we all followed in convoy to Noshka's large house, situated in its own grounds *somewhere* in the surrounding country, although I hadn't a clue where. I sat on a large settee with John on my right, whilst the tall, winking lady from the pub planted herself on my left. Noshka disappeared to get nibbles and drinks, whilst her husband put on some music, then sat opposite on a chair near the huge fireplace and stared. I learned that the person sitting on my left was called Jean; she worked on the buses and lived in Birmingham, which was fairly obvious from her pronounced

Brummie accent. It wasn't long before she extended a protective arm round my shoulder and I made no objection. It seems she knew Noshka and surreptitiously warned me to *be careful.* I wondered what I had to be careful of, but took her warning on board anyway.

The lights were dimmed, the drinks were flowing, the music was playing and men were shuffling around with men and women with women to the dreamy, seductive theme music from the film Bilitis. Jean asked me if I would dance, which I was pleased to do and might almost have felt romantically inclined, had I been foolish enough to dull my inhibitions with alcohol. The music stopped and we sat down on the huge settee again. It wasn't long before I realised someone's hands were caressing my legs. I looked at Jean, but knew it wasn't her because her right arm had crept round my shoulder again whilst she held a drink in her left hand. I leaned forward and looked down and was highly embarrassed to discover it was Noshka stroking my legs, while her husband looked on from his seat opposite.

Not wishing to cause a scene or seem unappreciative, I said politely, 'Do you mind Noshka. I don't think you're really my type.'

'I'll be anything you want me to be darling,' she whispered hoarsely.

Jean looked down at her and with alarming directness said, 'Fuck off Noshka, Lynn's with me!'

I extricated myself by asking if I could use the toilet, but when I emerged I was alarmed to see Noshka waiting on the landing. Without any preliminaries, she seized me in a lustful embrace and tried to plaster me with lipstick-laden kisses, the while she pleaded, 'You *will* stay the night won't you – promise me you'll stay the night.'

'Yes. Yes. I'll stay the night,' I promised, adding, 'I'd better find John to let him know what's happening.'

I struggled free from her unwelcome attentions and went to look for John, whom I eventually found necking with some chap in a corner.

'John! John!' I said urgently. 'Don't ask questions, we've got to get out of here – now!'

'Why?' he said. 'What's the hurry – I'm enjoying myself.'

'If you're enjoying yourself *that* much,' I hissed, 'stay - but you'll have to walk home - I'm off.'

'I'll come with you,' he said to my retreating back as I flew out of the hall door. I left the passenger door of my car open so that John could jump in quickly, but instead of John a huge boxer dog flew out of the house and jumped straight into the car, landing on my lap with a thud, and then started boisterously licking my face. 'Oh my God!' I mumbled, as I struggled to avert my face from the dog's unrestrained lickings. 'If it's not the lady of the house trying to kiss me to death its her dammed dog.'

John appeared – not a moment too soon – and I yelled at him, 'Get this bloody dog off me!'

He hauled the dog out of the car and we sped off into the night. I was sorry not to have had the chance to say cheerio to Jean, but I now knew why she'd warned me to be careful and I'm sure she would have understood the reason for my swift, unceremonious departure.

After this unnerving foray into the 'gay life', I decided seedy gay pubs and the people who frequented them were not really my scene and I was not anxious to repeat the experience in a hurry. To all outward appearances John and I were thought to be 'an item' which suited me very well. He was personable, fun to be with and a social asset with no strings, although I could have wished he didn't have quite such a liking for alcohol. He was never aggressive in his cups but tended to become maudlin and embarrassingly sentimental at times. He was also an ardent pill swallower, 'purple hearts' being his first choice. I remember an occasion when we went to Brighton and were sipping coffee in a sea-side café. I shook a couple of saccharin tablets into his palm to be used instead of sugar and watched in amazement as he threw the tablets into his mouth and took a sip of his unsweetened coffee to wash them down.

As we sat chatting I began to notice that he was turning a sickly yellow colour before my very eyes.

'Are you feeling all right John? I asked solicitously.

'Yes – I'm fine,' he assured me.

We continued to chat and I continued to stare at him, convinced he was going yellower and yellower.

'Are you *sure* you're alright?' I asked again.

'Of course I am!' he said. 'Why d'you keep asking me?'

'Because you look ever so ill to me. Your face has gone a funny colour and you look as if you've got yellow jaundice or something.'

I gave him my compact mirror and after examining his features for a few moments he burst out laughing. 'It's that instant suntan lotion you gave me to try out, before using it on yourself,' he said.

I was *so* relieved, not only because he wasn't seriously ill after all, but because I'd got him to experiment with it first. We dumped the bottle in the first bin we got to but it took a bit longer for John stopped looking jaundiced.

Chapter 46

Beware of Bewitching.

Now in my early forties I was still foot loose and fancy free (as the saying goes), contented with my life and successful in my work, with no desire to change anything that didn't need to be changed. So when Laura, a friend with whom I sometimes played tennis said she was having two friends visit from Devon and would I care to join them for a meal, I happily accepted the invitation, little knowing the impact this innocent invitation was to have on my life. I arrived bearing the obligatory bottle and was duly introduced to Mavis and Peggy. I learned throughout the evening that Peggy was the owner and head of a private preparatory school in Plymouth and Mavis was the housekeeper and looked after the children's welfare.

The evening went pleasantly enough and I was quietly pleased to note that Peggy seemed to hang on to my every word. She was an attractive person, slim, with corn blonde hair, a lively face and expressive brown eyes, and when it was time leave I had no hesitation at all in agreeing with the suggestion that we all meet up the following day to go out for a meal. In fact, I looked forward to our next meeting with more eagerness than I cared to admit, and if I'd made a favourable impression on the first meeting, I didn't want it to be less so on the second. So I took care with my make-up and general appearance, knowing that if I thought I looked nice, I would feel more disposed to *be* nice.

Perhaps I overdid it, for during the two weeks of their visit, I must have given the impression that there could be more to our new found friendship than I was willing to acknowledge. That I was attracted to Peggy was undeniable, but as far as I was concerned it was a pleasant interlude that would last only for the duration of their holiday, at the end of which she and Mavis would happily return to Plymouth and that would be the last I would see or hear of them. But things didn't work out that way and their visits to the Midlands became more frequent, sometimes staying with their friend Laura and then, because I had more room, occasionally staying with me. I have a natural instinct for being friendly and welcoming, a trait which has often been misconstrued and landed me in a situation in which I did not wish to find myself, but I never learned, and it was happening again.

Peggy, I discovered, had a very dominant and compelling personality and before I knew it, she was clandestinely trying to persuade me to give up my job and go to live with her and Mavis in Devon. I had no idea what Mavis's thoughts on the matter might be, but I protested that I couldn't possibly consider this, giving the genuine reasons that I didn't want to give up my job, and furthermore I didn't think her friend would take too kindly to the suggestion anyway.

There was something else I wanted to say but couldn't quite bring myself to say it, and that was that although I found her attractive, a few opportune, clandestine kisses and a bit of sly hand holding was not a sufficient basis for a lasting relationship, and certainly not one in which I might find myself in a subservient position in a *ménage a trois*.

I was even more dismayed when I subsequently received a letter to say that if I was not prepared to move to Devon she would put her house and the school on the market and move to Leamington. Knowing how slow the property market was at the time, I naively hoped it would be ages before this would happen, which would give her the opportunity to have a sensible re-think about her proposals. But *Sod's Law* intervened, and to my consternation, both properties sold within a few months. She bought Mavis a car and a small house in Saltash before upping sticks and arriving at my home with a fat bank balance, but no job and no home – save mine. I did my

166

best to be pleasant and welcoming, for I hadn't the heart or the guts to say that this was not what I wanted. It was too much, too soon and I felt trapped.

Mavis didn't take too kindly to the situation either, turning up at the house unexpectedly at odd hours of the day or night, making threats of various sorts, including one that she would sue for loss of livelihood and lifestyle. In the meantime, despite assiduously reading through the adverts in the Teacher's Supplement, there were no teaching jobs advertised in the area commensurate with Peggy's qualifications and experience, so rather than be idle, she took a temporary job with a car delivery firm.

It was a tough job with long hours and I felt sorry that she had been brought to this, especially when I couldn't live up to her expectations of me. But she got on well with the other drivers and it was not unusual for me to arrive home from work to find a few of her colleagues in the cottage, all chatting and laughing happily together. I never objected for I always felt more comfortable with a group of people, rather than being exclusive to one. It relieved me of the burden of being solely responsible for the happiness of another person. I think they thought I was just another visitor, for I remember an occasion when someone sitting next to me turned to me and said, 'I'm starving!'

'Oh, right,' I said, 'can I get you something to eat?'

She looked at me in surprise then said, 'D'you live here then?'

They sometimes had to drive what they called 'open chassis' which was not a very comfortable thing to do early on a cold, frosty winter morning. To protect themselves from the cold they were issued with thick black coats and sou'wester style head gear; thick, black woollen scarves to wind round the lower face and neck and goggles. We all laughed as Peggy regaled us with the incident of how she was walking along the road, thus attired, to pick up the open chassis, when a woman advancing towards her with a little girl clutching her hand said, 'Oh look darling – there's a bogey man.'

The job eventually came to an end when they began delivering the vehicles by huge car transporters, so Peggy was unemployed again and not very happy. Mavis was still being an absolute pain (and who could blame her) and I'm sure there must have been times when Peggy wondered if her hasty, life changing actions had all been worth it. I didn't think so but kept my thoughts to myself.

After scouring the advertisements for teaching posts and attending interviews all over the place, she finally landed a post as headmistress at a school in Worthing for children with learning difficulties. She wasn't sure whether to accept or not but it was the best paying job she'd been offered and after much soul searching decided to go for it.

So off she went, but not before extracting a promise from me that I would join her once she was settled. It seemed the least I could do - so I gave a half-hearted promise, heaved a sigh of relief and resumed my selfish, untrammelled life style.

Chapter 47

Nothing is Easy.

I sat in the lounge of the Metropole Hotel in Brighton sipping coffee whilst waiting for Peggy to arrive. I was not feeling as happy and excited as I should at the beginning of a week's holiday, for if I couldn't screw up the courage to say what had to be said now, it might never be said. And I knew that if I weakened, it would mean, not just the start of a holiday, but the beginning of a new life - since part of the holiday was to be spent visiting local estate agents. I did not want this commitment or financial involvement and neither was I prepared to be a dependant if I couldn't find a well paid job. But how could I tell her, in the least hurtful way, that despite everything she had given up for me, I still could not bring myself to sacrifice anything for her.

Lost in my thoughts and how best to articulate them, I was almost taken by surprise when Peggy suddenly appeared, all smiles and disarming charm. We ordered a couple of drinks and I raised my glass with an affected cheerfulness, then occupied myself studying the lunch menu in which I had no real interest.

Whilst waiting for the meal we conversed in a desultory manner, much as strangers might do whilst sitting in a doctor's or dentist's waiting room. Now was not the time…I didn't want to spoil her appetite.

After struggling to consume the meal I didn't really want we ordered coffee, over which I took my courage in my hands and said, 'Peg, I…um… don't really know how to say this…but…um…'

The words I'd carefully formulated in my mind had now deserted me, so I took a pull on my cigarette and a sip of the coffee to give me thinking time. She looked at me, long and hard, her eyes burning into my soul, and for a few brief seconds, I felt my resolve weakening.

I began again. 'Look Peg, I know this isn't what you want to hear but…'

'If I don't want to hear it – don't say it,' she cut in.

I jabbed my cigarette out in frustration, as if by so doing I was extinguishing the dying embers of my resolution, and was suddenly immersed in a spell of self-hatred.

I took another sip of my coffee, lit anther cigarette, leaned back in my chair, and began again.

'Peg,' I pleaded, 'I really have got to say it, so will you please try to understand?'

'There's no need,' she said, 'I *do* understand. I knew it was too good to be true.'

'Can we still be friends? I said lamely, 'and do you want to continue with the holiday?'

'It's up to you,' she said. 'I'll be staying anyway, at least until I've looked at the houses for sale I've ear-marked on this list.'

I felt a mixture of emotions: relief, guilt, compassion, tenderness and gratitude. 'I'd like to stay,' I said at last, feeling that was the least I owed her.

It was not an easy week. We tiptoed around each other, being overly polite and accommodating, she doing her best to hide her disappointment, me being as nice as I knew how to ameliorate it.

She found a house she liked at the right price in the right area and I was pleased. We parted company at the end of the week without blame or rancour, promising that we would keep in touch.

On my journey back to my home in Leamington I felt considerably more cheerful than I had on my outward journey, and even looked forward to getting back to the job I'd been on the verge of relinquishing. Nothing is for free though, and I paid for my freedom with a sense of guilt which I was never entirely able to master, not even when, to my relief, Peggy eventually found someone else with whom to share her life. Ross was a handsome, essentially kind hearted, though domineering woman, who was an interior decorator by day and ran a night club in the evenings. I think she and Peggy might have met when she was decorating Peggy's house. I can't say I liked her all that much, but I kept my thoughts to myself and would be forever grateful to her for coming into Peggy's life.

Chapter 48

Josie

Peggy and Ross visited me fairly often, when I would invite more friends round and have a party. Likewise, John and I would sometimes go to Brighton for the weekend. He liked Brighton and the 'gay life' so we often parted company when we arrived and he would go off and do his own thing, while I pursued much more ladylike activities, such as wandering round The Lanes and meeting up with people for elevenses or other such genteel activities more befitting to my sober tastes. However, I did sometimes accompany him to one of the many nightclubs that abound in Brighton, but although John was in his element, I never felt really comfortable in this sort of environment, although I did occasionally get to talk to some interesting people and one person in particular sticks in my mind. Her name was Josie, a middle-aged, lively person, who lived in Manchester but always came to Brighton for her holidays.

With a drink loosened tongue she told me all about herself. She lived with her lady friend in a council house in Manchester, but owned another house, which she used exclusively for work in her time honored profession. She had a great sense of humour and was very entertaining, and I listened, with an air of incredulity, as she explained how she managed to square her profession with her private life.

'Easy,' she said. 'I don't actually have sex with my clients. They're all kinky. Into bondage, flagellation, baby regression and a dozen and one other perversions that don't involve intimate contact.'

She told me one of her clients liked to dress up as a maid and clean the house from top to bottom. Part of the deal was that she must continually chastise and humiliate him for not doing his work properly, and insist that he did it all over again. For this strange pleasure he would reward her £100 an hour and her house was always spotless.

Another of her clients apparently had an even stranger fetish. He would arrive carrying a brief case and wearing a morning suit and a bowler hat. On arrival, he would solemnly divest himself of all his clothes save for his socks and the bowler hat.

Then, with equal solemnity, he would open his brief case to reveal six cream cakes which were handed over. She would have to pick up the cakes and walk six paces away then turn to face him. He would stand rigidly to attention in his socks and bowler hat and she would have to hurl the cream cakes, one at a time, at his manhood. If she scored a direct hit he would raise his hat and pay her an extra £10 for every cake that landed on target. She said she soon became an expert cream cake thrower, cream horns being her specialty.

I wondered how she'd got into prostitution and she told me her husband was a 'bullying bastard' and she determined that if she could find a way of leaving him she would. On a rare night out with one of her girl friends she met a man who seemed to take an interest in her. He bought her drinks and spoke kind words and asked if he could see her again.

She told him she was a married woman, but the next time she went to the pub he was there again. She felt quite flattered when he chatted her up again and told how stunning she looked when she was actually feeling quite dowdy, and after some hesitation, she finally agreed to meet him the following week. After a few drinks he drove to a lonely spot and when she half-heartedly resisted his amorous advances he surprised her by asking her if she wanted the money first. It didn't take her long to recover from the shock of his proposition and thereafter they met on her weekly night out and it escalated from there.

She was soon making more money on her night out than she made in a whole week as a cleaner, but she couldn't let her husband know what she was up to, so she saved the money and hid it in the base of her daughter's discarded doll's pram which stood in the garden shed with an innocent old doll safely tucked in on top of it.

It was her plan, when she'd saved enough, to leave her husband and take her child with her, but her escape from the marriage was precipitated earlier than she could have wished when a young friend of her daughter's came round to play. They were in the garden and without Josie noticing, the little girl had wheeled the doll's pram outside and tripped over the kerb. She looked out of the window to see what the yelling was about and saw the pram lying on its side and the money floating about in the breeze. Ignoring the prostrate crying child, she made a mad dash to rescue the floating fivers before the wind whisked them all away, but the game was up. Too many neighbours had seen the astonishing drama and helped in retrieving the money for it to be kept a secret from her husband any longer; so she fled with her daughter to her mother in Manchester and never went back to her husband. With the money she'd salvaged and some help from her mother she bought a house, which enabled her to pursue her new profession in style and comfort. Then she met a woman with whom she wanted to spend the rest of her life and found the happiness she'd never experienced in her marriage.

Chapter 49

Freda and Raymond

Through all the various phases of my life, I never lost my interest in, or love of horses and spent much of my spare time at the riding stables of Freda Newcombe. In her younger days she had been an expert and fearless rider, always smartly attired in her riding habit, and cut a fine figure on horseback. Her main claim to fame was that she had ridden twice on horseback from Lands End to John O'Groats, the first time alone, and the second time in company with six other riders and a dog. She had also completed the famous Dick Turpin ride from London to York, but I doubt that she would have done it in one night, as was claimed for the notorious Dick Turpin in the first half of the eighteenth century.

These exploits happened many years ago when she was a young woman. Now in her seventies, she had not grown old gracefully. Although, by no stretch of the imagination could she be described as being poor, she gave the appearance of being poverty stricken. She had become fat, a couple of her front teeth were missing, her face was lined and leathery and instead of the smart riding clothes of her younger years, she now looked more like an old bag lady and would often be seen in the most bizarre mixture of clothing. A pair of old fashioned jodhpurs on the lower half, shabby open sandals on sock-less feet, a grubby pink blouse that barely contained her ample bosom, over which she wore a man's loudly checked hacking jacket. All this incongruously topped with a fancy red hat from which poked recalcitrant wisps of greasy grey hair.

She bought all her clothes from second-hand or charity shops and wasn't too fussy as to whether they fitted her properly or not, just provided she felt she'd got a bargain. She once visited me wearing a very muddy pair of Wellington

175

boots. After planting herself down in an easy chair, she leaned back and crossed her legs and I couldn't help but notice that one boot seemed ever so much bigger than the other one.

'Why are you wearing one large boot and one normal size?' I asked.

'They were a bargain Gladys,' she said. (she called everyone *Gladys* including the boys) 'I got them from a shop in town. One is a size 7 and the other a size 11 so they let me have them for £2 - an absolute bargain!'

There were two cottages in the stable yard and she would live in one until it was too ramshackle to live in any longer, when she would move to the other cottage which would have been cleaned and put in reasonable order by some of the many children who spent their leisure hours at the stables. The process would start all over again when each cottage became fouled up. There were lots of valuable antiques in both these cottages but they could not be appreciated for they were all crowded in on each other and were almost always shrouded in a thick film of dust. Interspersed with the antiques, there was also a lot of rubbish, due mainly to her inability to resist a so-called *bargain.*

She would go along to the local auctions, bid for things she thought a bargain, then, because she didn't drive, would ask me, or anyone else with a vehicle mug enough to oblige, to go and pick up her *bargains,* which resulted at one time in her having four mattresses on one of her beds.

Despite her outrageous eccentricity, and often ill-tempered outbursts, children flocked to her stables, for hadn't she taught the parents of many of them to ride and even their grandparents before them, and, of course, these children were a willing source of free labour.

One of the children was a boy aged seven called Raymond. I noticed him particularly because he was so beautiful, with a shock of light coloured wavy hair, large hazel eyes framed with

176

long curling lashes, and the most appealing, childlike smile. He loved the horses and he loved Freda, old, scruffy and difficult as she was. I still remember the occasion when I once went round to the stables and found this beautiful child and this scruffy, weathered old woman, in the barn, lying flat on their backs on the hay, peacefully asleep. Another fond memory I have of them is when I called early one winter evening to give her a lift to some place or other. She was not at the house, so I went to the stables and found her and Ray in the tack room, snoring gently in unison, this time sitting in chairs with their legs stretched out before them. There was a fire in the black lead grate, on which Freda burned logs, but in this case, they were not really logs but un-sawn up small branches of trees, which, as the branch burned, it would be rammed further into the grate. Once again, I was moved by the sight of this young boy and old lady, sharing moments of love and relaxation, amid the pungent smell of leather, wood smoke and horse sweat.

As Ray got older and became an accomplished rider, Freda would allow him to lead rides, or at least assist in the leading of them. Randolph Turpin, one time middle weight boxing champion of the world, came to the stables to learn to ride. The first lesson went well, but the second time, although we only allowed him to walk, or at the most do a steady trot, this was obviously too tame for his liking. He got impatient, and despite advice to the contrary, he gave his mount a couple of sharp kicks in the ribs to make it go faster. Off the horse shot at full gallop, with Turpin completely out of control, and it didn't stop until it reached a high hedge, where it stopped so suddenly, it pitched him violently over the top. He was shaken but unscathed, and was sheepishly led back to the stables on a leading rein. When he'd gone, one of the children who'd been on the ride, with great relish related the incident and said, 'He wasn't hurt Miss Newcombe, but you should have seen his face – he went as white as a sheet.'

He didn't come riding again. His manager – George Middleton - deemed horse riding to be a much more dangerous sport than boxing!

One day, a new horse arrived at the stables. A handsome, three year old Appaloosa stallion whom she christened Chipper. This was because Chipperfield Circus had made their annual visit to town and she bought the horse from them – an absolute *bargain* she proclaimed. After a while, I suspected it was a bargain price because it wasn't quite right in the head and incapable of learning the routines and tricks expected of circus horses. It wasn't safe to take riders out on hacks and the only person able to ride it all was Raymond, who was now about thirteen or fourteen years old. He would go to the stables straight after school and Freda would feed him with very strange concoctions. On this occasion she gave him a tinned plum sandwich and offered one to me which I politely declined. She then decided to make a pot of tea, but after making it, discovered she hadn't any milk.

'Raymond,' she demanded. 'I want you ride to the corner shop on Chipper and fetch a bottle of milk, a pound of sausages, a packet of cream crackers and a bag of sugar.'

'How shall I carry them back?' he asked.

'Take this fishing basket,' she said. 'I got it from Locke & England's today for £1 – a bargain.'

Ray balanced the basket in front of him and trotted off, with Freda entreating him to hurry as she'd already brewed the tea and it was getting cold.

By the time he'd found someone to hold the horse whilst he went into the shop, then hold the basket whilst he re-mounted, the errand had taken much longer than Freda thought it should have done, and when he returned, mission safely accomplished, she charged towards him, berating him for taking so long. Then, as she tried to take the basket from him, Chipper reared up, she lost her grip on the basket and the contents spilled out onto the yard.

The bottle of milk smashed, the bag of sugar burst open, the dog ran off with the sausages and the only thing that remained intact were the cream crackers, but not for long, for they were crushed by Chipper's skittering hooves before they could be retrieved..

Freda roundly berated Ray, as if it was all his fault. He became flushed with un-spilled anger and cleared off home feeling justifiably aggrieved, leaving Freda shouting at me: 'These *people*, they don't know they're born Gladys! All they're fit for is bed work!'

I didn't quite know what that had to do with anything and it certainly didn't apply to Ray. Perhaps it was me she had in mind. Anyway, I thought I too would bid a hasty retreat before I was invited to share a pot of cold, over-brewed, sugarless and milk-less tea, with possibly a tinned plum sandwich thrown in for good measure.

Despite Freda's outrageous incongruity and eccentricity, she was still a well-loved character and it was a sad day when she decided to sell up and move back to her native Yorkshire where she spent her declining years with her brother and died in her nineties.

When Raymond left school he got a job with the Warwickshire Hunt where he remained until he was old enough to drive, when I took him on as a sales representative at the company I worked for. He is now in his early fifties; we remain good friends and he still comes to visit me from time to time.

Chapter 50

Weekends in Wales

Llandewi-Fach

It was also through my interest in horses that I first met Clare, and her husband Jonathan. They lived in a remote farmhouse on the Welsh Borders and I often visited at weekends, spending many happy hours riding the hills and the remote places of hidden Wales.

Sometimes J. came with us, (depending if he was able to get home from his army commitments) but more frequently we would be on our own. Having lived in the area for many years, there was little of the surrounding countryside with which Clare was not familiar and I was introduced to a new world of un-peopled spaces, far removed from the pressures and competitiveness of the working world of business in which I had my being.

I remember one occasion, whilst riding along a high ridge, looking down from this great height and seeing a tiny stone-built church, partially obscured by trees, nestling snugly in the valley below. There were no signs of other buildings, save for a farm, and I wondered where they would get their congregation from, if, indeed they ever had one. We carefully picked our way down the slopes and over a field until we reached the church, then tied the horses to some tree branches and went inside. The interior was plain and sparsely furnished, but had a certain charm, even if only because of its simplicity and remoteness. We peeped behind a curtain facing us as we entered and were surprised to see, amongst other things, an old wooden, hand carrying coffin bier, although, judging by the inscriptions on the gravestones, it was years since anyone had been buried here. Aside from the altar, which was draped in a plain white cloth, there was a pedal controlled harmonium facing us to the left and a pulpit near the window on the right.

Clare, being well versed in church music, managed to squeeze out some tunes on the ancient organ and, not to be outdone, I climbed up into the pulpit facing the door and sang the hymns to her accompaniment. Unbeknown to Clare, the door slowly opened and two people, a man probably in his forties and a boy of about twelve silently crept in. I kept on singing and Clare, unaware of their presence, continued to play the harmonium. The man and boy stood quietly for a few moments, before joining in the singing of *The Lord is my shepherd*. I smiled at them encouragingly and when we finished singing Clare swung round on the stool with a look of startled surprise.

'Good God!' she exclaimed. 'I thought we'd been joined by celestial voices from on high.'

We chatted with the visitors and discovered that the older man was accompanying his son on a twelve mile walk to enable him to get his Boy Scouts' athlete's badge. When they heard music emanating from the remote, tiny church, they said they just had to stop and investigate and the man said it was one of the loveliest things he'd experienced in years.

Chapter 51

Lost on the Brecons

On one of my visits to Wales Clare said she would take me to see the curtain waterfall at Ystrafelte in the Brecon Beacons. We set off in the early evening of a late summer day. She parked her car in the designated car park and we continued our journey on foot. I followed her through the wooded gorges and wet, slippery, sloping mountain paths until we reached the Sgwd Yr Eira curtain falls, and I thought how lucky I was to have such a strong, dependable friend, who seemed to know her way everywhere. I admired her strong athletic back and how she'd taken the sensible precaution of festooning her person with a lanyard from which hung a whistle, a stout penknife, and a compass, with a map and various other a aids in her haversack.

After a longish walk to get there, I stood, enchanted by the dramatic, breathtaking sight of frothy, snow white water, roaring over fifty foot high rocks and joyously plunging between high banks into the Afon Hepste below.

When I'd had my fill of admiring the awe-inspiring scene, Clare decided that in view of the wet, slippery conditions of the sloping woodland path, and the fast failing light, it would not be safe to go back the way we'd come. She said we would have to cross the river on the narrow stone path that ran behind the fall, to take a safer route back.

Suddenly, the falls lost their charm and beauty and became brutal and terrifying. Never having learned to swim, the very idea of walking behind that watery curtain filled me with fear and I stood my ground. Besides, I'd only that morning been to the hairdressers and didn't want to mess up my hair by getting soaked. Despite my protestations, Clare crossed over expecting me to follow – but I wouldn't. It was no longer a question of

182

"Wither thou goest I will go." She shouted above the roar of the cascading water, 'Right! You go back the way we've come then and I'll go back this way.'

Given my appalling sense of direction, the thought of being lost in slippery wooded gorges was even more scary than the alternative, so I screwed up my courage and crossed over, arriving on the other side shivering and wet but with a mild sense of triumph, and as we clambered up out of the steep gorge I was assured by Clare there was a road at the top of it. There *was* no road. 'It must be at the top of the next hill,' she said.

We struggled to the top of the next hill... no road.

Unfazed, she assured me it would be at the top of the next mountain, by which time I began to doubt her navigational skills. 'Clare,' I protested. 'I don't think there's anything at the top of that mountain except more bloody mountain!'

She gave me a withering stare then said, 'In that case we're lost.'

Darkness was rapidly descending and we floundered about on the mountain for ages, following narrow paths which always turned out to be animal tracks that led to nowhere. I wasn't enjoying the adventure anymore and had quietly become resigned to spending the night on the mountain with the possibility of dying of exposure. Then suddenly, in the far distance, I glimpsed the lights of a car.

'I've seen the lights of a car,' I called out to Clare, (who was occupied turning her map upside down and trying to consult her compass by torchlight) 'and I don't care what your map or compass says, I'm going to keep walking in *that* direction. At least we know there's a road.'

We stumbled on in the direction of the glimpsed car light, regardless of the sometimes treacherous, bog-bound terrain, until we finally reached the remote, narrow country road. We walked along the deserted road until we reached a pub called

The Lamb at Penderyn. After ordering a couple of drinks and two packets of crisps we asked if they could tell us the way to the Curtain Falls car park and how far it was.

They gave us directions (which Clare immediately understood) but my heart sank when they said it was about eleven miles.

'Is there a bus?' I asked.

'Bus?' repeated my informant. 'Bus – no, you won't get a bus round yer this time of night.'

'What about a taxi?' I asked brightly.

'Taxi?' They looked at us as if we were from another planet, then added, 'No. No taxi's round yer. You'll have to walk.'

We walked, but at least we now knew that we were walking in the right direction and Clare said, according to her calculations it was more like seven miles than the eleven we'd been told. Considerably heartened, we began to sing to aid our steps, until we saw a house in the distance and Clare told me to shut up in case we disturbed the residents. We laughed as we drew nearer and discovered it wasn't a house but a small chapel at the entrance to a cemetery.

'We'd have a job to disturb that lot,' she quipped, so we kept singing until we finally ran out of breath and tunes. It was a relief when we found the car park and began our journey back over the Brecons, although misadventure hadn't entirely done with us even then. A fog had descended and as we picked our way along the narrow strip of mountain road, through the mist we barely discerned a herd of wild ponies crossing. We managed not to collide with them but one of the foals reared up in alarm and as he came down he got Clare's wing aerial stuck up his nose. I got out to calm the foal whilst she retracted the aerial and as far as we could ascertain, no damage was done to animal or car.

It was well past midnight when we got back and we were starving, so I heated up the cauliflower cheese I'd made earlier.

Clare ate it so quickly that she was promptly sick afterwards and vowed she would never eat cauliflower cheese again – which was a pity, as it's one of the few meals in my limited cooking repertoire that I'm really good at and Jonathan always enjoyed it.

Chapter 52

Growing Tomatoes.

The farm cottage where Clare and Jonathan lived had two large paddocks, on which nothing grew except grass. I thought it a bit of a waste to have all this ground and not actually grow anything, but Clare jokingly labelled herself *congenitally incapable of growing and nurturing things*, and Jonathan, being away a lot on his army commitments, confined his gardening activities to mowing the grass and keeping the hedges nicely trimmed.

I did not have much in the way of gardening experience myself at that time, but someone gave me a tray of tomato plants, so I took them with me on my next visit.

Clare eyed them doubtfully, but encouraged by Jonathan's acquiescent smile, I took them outside, followed by Clare, who indicated where she thought would be a suitable spot for them. Eager to get them planted, I toiled with my trowel in the heavy rain and unyielding clay soil at the foot of the hedges in the shadiest part of the garden. It was not easy, but I finally got all six plants dug in and felt quite pleased with my efforts.

Thereafter, if I had a phone call, it wasn't a polite enquiry as to their well-being, my primary interest being in the tomato plants and their progress. So I would frequently say, 'Hello, how are the tomato plants getting on?'

The discouraging reply would invariably be, 'Still alive, but not exactly thriving.'

'Have they got any flowers on them yet?'

'Not yet, but I think there are a few buds.'

'Great! I read somewhere that if you talk to plants they do much better, so why don't you try talking to them.'

'Don't know what to say.'

'If you don't know what to say try singing to them. I'm sure it will be just as effective.'

So Clare promised to sing to them and in the fullness of time, the flowers came and eventually transformed themselves into hard, green, pea-like spheres, in which state they appeared to remain forever. High summer came and went and the telephoned report on progress of the tomatoes was dishearteningly negative (despite all the alleged singing).

Negative, that is, until one happy week-end visit when, on arrival, I was led out to the paddock to look at the tomato plants. There they stood, in all their red-ripe glory, the branches bent over and groaning with the weight of the tomatoes dangling from them.

'Oh! How marvellous! How absolutely marvellous,' I gushed, as I clasped my hands together in delight, then stretched them forth to pluck a few.

Clare hauled me backwards, warning, 'Don't touch them.'

'Why ever not?' I said. 'They're just right for picking.'

Shrugging off Clare's restraining hand on my shoulder, I advanced a little closer. It was only then that I saw that the lovely ripe tomatoes were all tied onto the branches with black cotton.

I really appreciated the humour, but decided growing tomatoes was perhaps best left to people who knew about these things and I never tried to grow them again.

Chapter 53

Five Old Ladies and a Boat.

In my all too few idle moments of solitude, I realised that outside of my demanding job, I seldom had time to settle into the rust of routine, trying, as I was to please everybody who needed me, yet remain aloofly independent. I valued my freedom, but sometimes pondered – am I really free. For the freedom I valued so highly was really only the freedom to be available for other people.

So when, on one of my visits to Brighton, I learned that Peggy had been diagnosed with throat cancer, I experienced a visceral shudder of compassion and spent much of my free time over the next few months travelling to Brighton. It was sometimes irksome and always distressing to see her so ill, for there were many unexpected complications as a result of the treatment, but I felt it was the least I could do to try and help her through this harrowing time.

She eventually got well enough to return to her job, but due to further complications finally had to give it up and take early retirement. When she felt well enough, she and Ross came to stay with me in Leamington. We went out for Sunday lunch, together with Gwen and Winifred, a couple of friends of mine from Cheltenham to a restaurant at Preston Bagot which stood on the banks of the Grand Union canal. It was a sunny, pleasant day, and as we watched the canal boats chug slowly by Peggy wistfully said, 'Isn't this peaceful. Wouldn't it be lovely to have a holiday on a canal boat.'

'Just what I was thinking,' chimed Gwen. 'I've been trying to persuade Lynn to do this for ages – haven't I Winifred?'

'Yes dear,' she said, with her customary acquiescence.

I had serious misgivings about the viability of five old ladies crewing a large canal boat without a modicum of experience between us, but finally succumbed to the persuasive entreaties of the others. And as I was the only one who lived locally, I was detailed to visit the Warwick Boat Yard the following day to see if there were any dates available. At this late stage I thought (even hoped) it would be a pretty futile quest, and was surprised when they said they had one week at the beginning of July. I phoned the others with the news and so it was that the five of us turned up at Kate Boat Yard in Warwick to begin our holiday.

There was Peggy, retired headmistress, in her sixties and still bravely battling with the effects of throat cancer; her friend Ross, interior decorator and proprietor of a night club in Brighton, who, at fifty-five, was the youngest, biggest and bossiest but who complained of a dodgy back. Then there was Winifred, a retired midwife, who'd recently had an operation for a brain aneurism which had seriously impaired her memory, and her friend Gwen, also a retired midwife, who had mild angina, clinical depression and a querulous nature. Then of course there was me, a now retired branch manager, who, at sixty-five was the eldest, healthiest and most lithe of our motley crew of five.

Despite my doubts, I had to admit to a grudging sense of adventure as we boarded the boat, struggling with a mountain of black bin bags, which Ross had suggested we use instead of suit cases, on the grounds they would take up less room. We examined the interior of the boat, which revealed a dining area towards the front which somehow converted into beds when rearranged and which Gwen and Winifred promptly bagged as their sleeping quarters. In the middle of the boat was the galley, opposite which was a tiny shower room and next to that was a revolting chemical toilet. Towards the rear of the boat was a sitting area which also converted into a double bed where

Peggy and Ross elected to sleep, and I was allocated the only remaining sleeping place, which was a two foot wide bunk immediately above them and fixed to the wall of the boat.

After being briefly instructed on how to handle the boat, we set off on our adventure. We were modest in our ambitions, making Stratford-on-Avon our final destination, which was actually only nine miles away by road. We thought how nice it would be moor the boat in the canal basin on the edge of the town and spend a few days looking around, shopping, eating at the many inviting restaurants and perhaps even going to the theatre. All this without the worry of where to park a car, which, in this popular tourist town, was nigh on impossible. I remember once seeing a road sign which stated 'You are now entering Shakespeare Country' underneath which some wag had added, 'Where **parking** is such sweet sorrow.'

Ross had already bought herself a fake, peaked naval officer's cap and assumed the role of Captain and decreed that she and Gwen would do the locks. Peggy volunteered to be the cook. Winifred, not being quite in her right mind, was told to relax and enjoy herself, whilst I was consigned to the unsheltered platform from where I steered the boat.

It was with some trepidation that I approached the first lock as I'd only just come to terms with the art of steering, but I was pleased to find that I'd managed to keep the boat straight and face the lock square on. I slipped the gear into neutral to await the opening of the lock, but had not bargained for the strong cross-wind that skewed the boat to a crazy sideways angle.

Ross yelled, 'What the hell are you playing at?'

Fearful and frustrated, I yelled back, 'I'm doing my best, but the steering isn't working.'

It took me a while to realise that the steering only worked when the engine was engaged, so after slipping it back into gear (why hadn't the man at the boatyard told us this, or perhaps he had and in the welter of information it had been forgotten).

Anyway, we sailed safely through the lock without further ado and negotiated a couple more before reaching the famous Hatton flight of twenty-one locks in a distance of less than two miles.

At this point Peggy, who had stayed with me on the steering platform, now disappeared into the bowels of the boat, but not before hurting my feelings by saying: 'Why haven't you got the guts to admit that you're not actually enjoying yourself?'

It was too early to decide whether I was enjoying myself or not, so I didn't answer, went into a brief sulk and concentrated on the task ahead.

Meantime, Ross and Gwen were furiously unwinding and re-winding the lock gates, whilst I valiantly endeavoured to hold my nerves and the boat steady whilst incarcerated in the never ending tomb-like locks. There were lots of people on the tow path, shouting instructions and advice, which I gratefully accepted then mostly forgot. At some stage I became aware of a middle-aged man and a younger man on the tow path who seemed to be following our progress. The older man asked if we would like any help and I swallowed my pride and said, 'Yes please.'

He clambered on board and the younger man went to help Ross and Gwen with the endless winding of the locks. Just as well, for they looked to be in a state of near collapse. I was a bit wracked myself, but more from fear and nervous tension than physical effort.

Nice man put his hand out and said, 'I'm Jim.'

'Good to meet you, Jim,' I beamed. 'I'm Lynn. It's a relief to have someone on board who knows what they're doing.'

He stood with me on the steering platform chatting encouragingly but resisted the temptation to take over, thereby leaving my sense of achievement and importance intact.

After emerging from the twenty-first lock, the two men left us to our own devices, but not before I gave them fulsome thanks for their help. Then Peggy reappeared from where she'd taken refuge inside the boat and cautioned me, 'You shouldn't have welcomed a strange man on board and you were being much too friendly,' she said, wagging an admonishing finger at me as if I was one of her erstwhile pupils, then added less sternly, 'After all – you never know.'

'Hmn, at my age, I should be so lucky,' I retorted.

Shortly after leaving the last of the locks, we found a place to moor for the night. Gwen volunteered to be the 'banger-in' of the mooring stakes and said she would tie up as she remembered how the man at the boat yard had showed us how to do the knots. But she hadn't remembered at all and Ross started berating her for her ineptitude. She got a bit tearful and we all became fractious and impatient, except, that is, for Winifred, who stood around looking slightly bemused and wondering what the fuss was all about.

I was once a Girl Guide and had a badge for tying knots so I tried my hand at it and had a measure of success, but every time I got one tied, Ross decreed that the stake was in the wrong place, so out they would come and the stake banging-in would start all over again.

Gwen got fed-up, refused to do any more banging and sat on the bank and cried. I felt sorry for her and went over and whispered, 'Don't cry Gwen. You know what a bossy bugger she is. I'll do the banging if you will hold the stakes and it will be my fault if they're in the wrong place.'

She sniffed her last snivel and came back to join us.

'Before we start, where do you suggest we put the stake Ross?' I asked in my most placatory voice.

'Stick it where you bloody like,' she snarled. 'I've had enough.'

So I stuck it where I bloody liked. Gwen held on to it and I brought the hammer high and accidentally banged Ross on the head, then brought it crashing down on Gwen's thumb.

Ross yelped and held her head (no blood) and Gwen squealed and nursed her thumb (a lot of blood). I was distraught and shouted at them both, 'Sorry! Bugger the boat. I never wanted to come on it in the first place.'

We all stood around looking miserable. Ross gingerly fingered the lump on her head. Peggy put a plaster on Gwen's bleeding thumb; Winifred quietly stood watching and I felt foolish, frustrated and contrite all in one, and still the boat hadn't been secured. Then, as if by magic, our two nice men from the tow path reappeared and in no time at all knocked in the stakes in the right places and had us expertly tied up in our moorings. They went their way and after we'd washed and tidied ourselves up, we walked across some fields to the Waterman Inn where we were able to relax over a drink, a good meal and restore ourselves to our rightful minds. There also, were our two nice gentlemen who asked if they could join us.

As usual, it was left to me to be pleasant and do all the chatting, but Jim wouldn't hear of it when I tried to buy them a drink as a little 'thank you' for all their help, and insisted on buying us one instead. We learned they were father and son, lived locally and the son's name was Steve. They told us they liked being on the tow path when they weren't at work and when I said how grateful we were for their help they assured me it was a great pleasure and they enjoyed doing it. I warmed to them and secretly hoped we would we would see them again on our return journey.

Back on the boat we spent a frenetic half hour or so sorting out our bedding and converting daytime areas into sleeping quarters. I eyed my bunk which was too high up on the wall for me to take a flying leap, so Ross gave me a leg up with such enthusiasm that I hit my head on the top of the boat, which made me feel better about hitting her on the head with the hammer.

We all slept surprisingly well, although I was careful how I turned over in case I tumbled out and landed on Ross and Peggy below. I woke at 6am and was desperate to go to the toilet but couldn't work out how I could get down, unaided, without disturbing them. After much thought I decided that if I sat on the edge of the bunk, slithered for a little and then leapt, I would land in the space beyond them. But the space was too narrow and on landing I bumped into the side of the boat, bounced back and landed on my bottom on Peggy's face.

She cried out in terror and Ross shouted, 'What the hell's going on?'

I almost wet myself laughing before reaching the toilet. Fortunately, they saw the funny side of it too after they'd recovered from the shock. And so began our second day.

SATURDAY

The commotion and laughter woke Gwen and Winifred but they, like Ross and Peggy, elected to stay in bed a bit longer. Being unable to get back to my bed unaided, even if I'd wanted to, I got washed and dressed in peace after which I redeemed myself by taking them all a cup of tea in bed. Then I left the boat to investigate the surrounding countryside, eerily clothed, as it was, in early morning mist. I found a suitably secluded spot and squatted behind a bush to perform the second part of my morning ablutions, then walked on, enjoying the solitude and stillness of early morning.

When I got back everyone was astir, and after eating the fried breakfast Peggy had cooked for us we sorted ourselves and the boat out and finally cast off about eleven o'clock and had a delightful, lock-free cruise of a mile or more. I wanted to do some filming so Ross took over the steering and I went to the front of the boat. Soon we entered a long dark tunnel and I was hoping to film our emergence into glorious sunshine at the other end. Camera at the ready and eye to the view finder, I was suddenly drenched by an avalanche of water cascading through the tunnel roof. I dashed headlong back inside the boat, tripped over something and went sprawling into the dining table where Gwen and Winifred were sitting waiting to resume their game of cards. They were not pleased when the cards went flying in all directions.

Ross, in the meantime, could not leave her post at the tiller and got soaked to the skin before Peggy remembered we had an umbrella on board, which Ross ungraciously spurned, saying, 'Too bloody late – I'm already drenched.'

I thought it was funny but no one else was laughing, so I quickly straightened my face and, having checked that my camera hadn't suffered any damage, pretended to be as discomforted as they obviously were. Ross wanted to get out of her wet clothes so I took over the steering again. Shortly, I noticed a small bridge and wondered if I should turn left under it or carry straight on. (There should be signs for fools like us). The way ahead was broad and more inviting than the narrow strip of water under the bridge, so we steamed on, although I wasn't too sure we were doing the right thing.

After a while, I saw a fisherman on the bank and called out, 'Excuse me, are we going in the right direction for Stratford?'

'No,' he said. 'You're on your way to Birmingham. You should have turned off at the bridge and got onto the Stratford canal.'

My heart sank when I realised the width of the water we were presently in was less than the width of the boat. 'Oh my God!' I groaned. 'How the hell do I turn the boat around here?'

'Carry on for about a mile,' he said, 'and you'll come to a *turning pool*. Come back on yourselves and turn right under the bridge.'

'Cheers,' I said, as I gave him a thumbs-up and chugged off to the turning pool.

Before reaching it, we found a mooring place at Lapworth, so Peggy and I left the boat to look for a grocery shop to stock up with some food. After quite a bit of walking we were hot and thirsty so we stopped at a pub we'd noticed on our way out. We got chatting to the locals and when we told them we were on a canal boat they became really friendly and bought us a drink and gave us lots of advice and it was difficult to get away. We had a really pleasant half hour or so, but for a reason which escapes me, we decided not to tell the others what we'd been up to. When we got back, our good humour was quickly dispelled when the others rounded on us and demanded to know what had taken us so long.

'It took us ages to find a shop,' I lied, 'and the bags were so heavy we had to keep stopping for a rest.' Ross's retort was neither worthy of record or reply. Suffice to say that goodwill was quickly restored after we'd enjoyed a nice lunch, cooked, as usual, by Peggy, herefforts appreciated all the more knowing that she couldn't eat the food herself, restricted, as she was, to soup or other liquid food only.

After lunch we set off again, sailing happily along in a rare spell of fine weather until we reached a large expanse of water. I was entranced with its beauty as the sunlight danced and glistened on the rippled water, so much so that when Ross and Gwen jumped off the boat to open the first of six locks in a row, I mindlessly steered the boat through, secretly congratulating myself on my improving skill and confidence and feeling rather pleased with myself. Pleased – that is – until I suddenly realised the broad expanse of water I'd so lavishly admired was actually the pool in which we should have turned round.

'Oh no! I don't believe it,' I wailed.

'What's up now?' the others chorused.

'We shouldn't have come through these locks,' I said. 'We should have turned round before we got to them. That lovely expanse of water was the turning pool.'

I was furious with myself, not to mention worried as to how I was going to manage to steer backwards through the locks. Once more, Peggy disappeared into the bowels of the boat with Winfred, whilst Ross, Gwen and I spent the next few minutes blaming each other for our stupidity. Of course, I might have been more alert if I hadn't had a couple of drinks at the pub, but I wasn't going to confess to that!

Once again, some people on the tow path came to my aid. This time, an elderly gentleman and his wife. Following the gentleman's instructions, I managed to back out of the first two locks and found myself in wider water, where I was able to turn the boat around to face the right way. The couple continued to follow our progress and I noticed they had a very ancient, frail looking lady with them who announced she was 'fed-up' with standing around. I invited her onto the boat, sat her on a deck chair and accidentally knocked off her large-brimmed hat. She was not amused, especially when I was unable to stifle a giggle as I apologised and handed it back to her. Meanwhile, the lady and gentleman continued to follow us along the tow path, shouting encouragement until we were finally out of the last lock. Then he suggested that as we were near a watering hole, it might be a good idea to fill our water tanks. Ross took charge of this, but the hose snaked out of her hands and she accidentally soaked the gentleman with water.

We were shocked, chorused our apologies and thought it poor reward for all the help they'd given us.

'Don't worry. It's made his day,' his wife assured us, as they helped frail lady off the boat.

'Did you enjoy your little trip?' I asked solicitously.

'No. I don't like boats,' she said sourly.

We waved our lovely helpers goodbye and had a serene, lock and trouble free journey back to where we should have been and turned right under the bridge onto the Stratford Canal. At about 8.30pm we came across a designated mooring place which was right outside the Fleur de Lys pub at Lowsonford. We tied the boat to the already existing stakes and made our way to the pub. I knew this place well, for after the war, when food was still on ration, they were renowned for their delicious steak and kidney pies and people came from far and wide to sample them.

The pub was full, but we managed to find seats next to two American couples who were touring by car. They thought Britain was *awesomely beautiful* but confessed they were terrified of the break-neck speed of our drivers on what they called our narrow roads.

Back on the boat we enjoyed an evening meal of dumpling stew which had already been prepared by Peggy.

SUNDAY

We left our moorings about 10am in torrential rain which continued all day. Peggy insisted on staying on the steering platform with me, although, given the state of her health, I would have been much happier if she stayed dry inside the boat and left me to suffer alone. Then she decided it wasn't fair that Ross and Gwen should do all the hard work at the locks and suggested I change jobs with Ross and give her a spell at the steering. Anxious to keep the peace and mindful of the fact that she had insisted on paying for me to be on this trip, I willingly agreed.

Given Gwen's experience with the opening and shutting of the locks and my lack of it, I was content for her to take charge and after heaving and tugging on the windlass in accordance with her instructions I began to worry when nothing seemed to happen.

'Are you sure we're turning it the right way?' I asked Gwen.

She clasped her hands to her head and cried out, 'Oh my God, I don't know what I'm supposed to be doing.'

I gave her a belligerent stare, then realised she must be having one of her panic attacks, so I fled back to the boat to report to Ross that Gwen didn't know what she was doing, so how was I supposed to know.

With a sigh of resigned superiority, Ross left the steering platform and went back to the locks and I resumed my post at the helm. Peggy accused me of being unfair to Ross, turned sour on me and we didn't speak for the next three hours. Meanwhile, Gwen seemed to be at the end of her tether and was thoroughly fed-up with the lot of us. Winifred was the only one unaffected by all the drama and prevailing ill-humour. She remained inside the boat, emerging from time to time with a vacuous smile and repeating: 'Isn't it lovely. It's something I've always wanted to do.'

It was time for something to eat and we moored up at the Haven Tea Rooms, Preston, the very place where the idea for our crazy venture had first been conceived. Then – the boats were slowly chugging along in brilliant sunshine and all was peace and joy and everyone except me thought what a wonderful idea when Peggy suggested we try to book a canal holiday.

The rain continued to pour down as we sat in the café, wet, miserable and argumentative to the point of being quarrelsome and I was embarrassed to think what the other diners must have thought about us – five scruffy old ladies squabbling like a flock of fretting starlings.

Back on the boat an uneasy peace broke out and we all agreed we would try to make it to Stratford by nightfall. Peggy, when she wasn't down in the galley preparing food, stoically remained at the helm with me and kept urging me to go faster, but I refused as we would have exceeded the maximum speed limit of four miles an hour. This brought further disapproval from her and hurt and angry silence from me.

Meanwhile, Ross was berating Gwen for dropping her windlass into the canal and she was once more reduced to tears. We learned later that this sort of thing happened quite frequently and that they could easily be retrieved with a boat hook.

By 7pm soaked and tired, we realised we wouldn't reach Stratford that evening after all, so we moored between some locks at Wilmcote. More problems ensued, as, due to the profusion of Indian Balsam and Rosebay Willowherb that had colonised the banks, it was difficult to get the boat close enough for the less agile to make a leap from the boat onto the towpath, or walk the narrow plank which had thoughtfully been provided. After a great deal of struggle, we finally managed to get close enough to the bank, but then Peggy decided it wasn't. At this, I finally lost my cool and shouted, 'Well if this isn't good enough, you can damn-well start all over again but without any help from me!'

The boat remained where it was and nothing more was said. We struggled out of our soaking wet clothes and hung them up in the tiny shower cubicle, which left no room to use the place for the purpose intended, so we just towelled ourselves down and got into some dry clothes. A nice meal on the boat and a couple of bottles of wine later we were feeling quite human again and were even able to laugh at some of the miseries of the day. Since it was still raining hard we didn't leave the boat that evening and decided instead, to watch the black and white television, but reception was so bad, we gave up and played cards.

Then we became aware of a strange *ticking* sound. Despite all the rain and the fact that we'd recently topped up at a watering hole, Ross decided that our water was too low. We had been warned the pump would *tick* if this happened. With her usual tendency to over-react to any given situation, Ross forbade us to use water for any purpose whatsoever – not even to make a cup of tea.

'Not even a cup of tea?' Winifred absently queried.

'No. Not even a cup of tea.' Ross repeated.

Winfred shrugged her shoulders and sighed, 'Oh well, we shall just have to drink water then.'

Ross gave her a withering look, Gwen told her not to be so bloody stupid and Peggy and I locked eyes and dared to smile. There followed an inquest as to who might have left a tap running and if we were all to be believed, none of us had. I knew it wasn't me for I hadn't made a drink or even had a shower since we started this trip, so when I was legged up to my bunk I got into bed with a clear conscience and slept the sleep of the just.

.MONDAY

I woke up at about 6 o'clock as usual and considered going for my customary morning walk. I rubbed the condensation from the window (or should it be port hole) and peered out to discover it was still raining; also that the boat had drifted some distance from the bank. To get the plank out would have caused too much disruption and besides, I didn't fancy walking it alone. So I decided to snuggle down again, forgot how narrow the bunk was and as I heaved myself over I fell out, startling Ross and Peggy out of their wits – yet again. They were not amused but managed to see the funny side of it later.

Getting back into the bunk was not an option, so, mindful of the water situation, I threw some clothes on without bothering to wash; and being unable to leave the boat was obliged to use the detestable chemical toilet. I sat quietly in the boat wondering why on earth I'd allowed myself to be talked into this holiday, knowing beforehand that as a group we were not really compatible.

Gwen could argue for England and Peggy would never be gainsaid. Ross was bossy and over-bearing and Winifred was mostly *non compos*. I expect I had my faults too but God knows – I couldn't think of any. But I did try to keep the peace and please everyone, probably pleasing no one in the end.

At about 7.30 am the others began to stir, disturbing my reverie, and Ross graciously gave permission for the water to be switched on so that we could have a cup of tea with our breakfast. I think she might have been lynched if she hadn't.

The rain continued to pour down relentlessly and before we prepared to cast-off Ross came up with the brilliant idea of using the black bin bags we'd brought with us to protect us from the wet. She cut holes for our heads and arms and wound the bags round our legs and tied us up with string. So now I know what it's like if you're into bondage,' I quipped. No one laughed.

Rain, lack of water for our ablutions and rude awakening notwithstanding, we were all in surprisingly good humour and ready to face the day. I estimated that Stratford was, at most, now only about three hours cruising time away and we were looking forward to getting there. At 9am we were all geared up and ready to go. Ross went through the normal procedures to get the engine started with me confirming instructions viz: make sure engine stop is pushed in; engine is out of gear; accelerator is slightly advanced; key is in ignition; count fifteen then pull the starter to ignite.

Gwen had bravely walked the plank to untie the ropes; I was eager at the helm to move off and Ross was all set to get off the boat and help Gwen with the next lock. Nothing happened. We followed the procedure once more – still nothing happened. Then came the realisation – the battery was flat. A few unladylike expletives followed before Ross and I decided we would need to get professional help.

We walked along the tow path until we came to an isolated, tumbledown cottage and fought our way through a tangle of bramble and weeds to reach the front door. We knocked but got no reply so we knocked again more loudly. The door was angrily flung open by a terrifying young man with black eyes blazing out of a white face which was partially obscured by a bushy, matted beard and framed with a mass of frizzy, unkempt black hair. Before being given a chance to enquire if he had a telephone he told us to 'Fuck off,' Needless to say we did – very quickly.

After walking for a further mile or so, we saw a farmhouse in the distance to our left and made our way across the field to it. As we neared, we were alarmed by three huge, furiously barking dogs leaping at us, which alerted the farmer to our presence. He called the dogs off and after we'd explained our predicament he allowed us to use his telephone to ring Kate Boat Yard. We told them our problem, gave them our location and they promised to be with us in half an hour.

As we made our way back to the boat I looked at Ross in amazement. 'Half an hour. Half an hour,' I repeated. 'D'you realise its taken us three days to get this far and they'll be with us in half an hour!'

'Idiot!' she said good naturedly, 'they'll be coming by car not boat.'

In the event it was over two hours before they finally reached us and fitted another battery. After investigation it was discovered that the 'hot wire' had burned out, preventing the charge from getting through. More delay whilst the mechanic went off to fetch the required part. Before leaving he assured us that we weren't short of water. The mysterious ticking we'd heard the night before was the battery running down.

It was gone one o'clock by the time the problem was finally fixed. We'd had the good sense to keep our bin bags on, for after a short spell of sunshine the heavens opened again. I was beginning to worry about Peggy who was looking increasingly frail, though uncomplaining. Despite being so unwell, she insisted on staying at the helm with me. Ross and Gwen continued to toil at the locks and Winifred would occasionally appear from below and go through her, 'Isn't it lovely,' routine, then disappear again to continue playing her endless games of Patience.

After about three hours we finally reached Stratford-on-Avon. The rain had stopped, the sun was shining and the town park, adjacent to the canal basin, was awash with colourful, beautifully cared for flower beds. Swans and rowing boats glided gracefully along the river Avon that ran alongside. We'd often visited Stratford in the past and enjoyed the tourist attractions, but we were now a bit of a tourist attraction ourselves, as people watched our progress through a difficult, narrow lock and into the broad basin where we moored the boat in one of the few remaining spaces. There were lots of Japanese about at the ready with their cameras to snap our every move and I hoped I wouldn't make a total ass of myself whilst trying to manoeuvre the boat into the narrow berth. Fortunately, I managed this reasonably well and only slightly banged the boat alongside. I wasn't sure whether there was anyone on board, but if there was, no one came out to complain that I'd sent their crockery flying or anything.

We quickly divested ourselves of the bin bags, smartened ourselves up and those of us accustomed to wearing make-up applied it, then all emerged, smiling and happy. Peggy and Ross went into town to do some shopping and the rest of us stayed with the boat and ate ham sandwiches and I quite enjoyed being gawped at by the many visitors milling around. When Peggy and Ross returned they went off to the local swimming baths and, though no swimmer myself, I wished I'd had the forethought to bring a bathing costume as it would have been nice to flounder about in the shallow end and feel clean again. As it was, I contented myself with having a wash in the public conveniences, then went back to the boat and dangled my dirty feet in the canal.

Gwen took the opportunity, during the absence of the others, to complain about them. She was convinced nobody liked her and I felt she had some justification for feeling this way, even if it wasn't true. Ross would order her to get back on the boat between locks, Peggy would want to know what she was doing on the boat when she should be helping Ross, and I would tell her she was in the way if she ventured up onto the steering platform. If she went inside the boat, poor Winifred got on her nerves with the frequent repetition of her 'Isn't it lovely,' routine, and on one occasion I heard Gwen snap back, 'It isn't lovely Winifred, it's anything but bloody lovely!'

'Yes dear,' said Winifred in resigned tones.

I tried to mollify Gwen by saying that if she did as Ross asked her in the first place without arguing and being so contentious it would make things a lot easier. We had, after all, agreed that Ross should be captain, so it was up to us to do as we were told. I conceded that Peggy was sometimes a bit hard on her, but then, she snapped at us all at least once a day. Most of the time I managed to ignore it as she was not a well woman and was frightened a lot of the time, especially when we were deep in the locks. She said it made her feel as if she was buried in a tomb.

. I reminded Gwen I wasn't keen to come on this trip in the first place, but that I was trying to make the best of it and there were times when I was even enjoying myself - in a masochistic sort of way. So why didn't she try to relax and do the same and stop whingeing all the time.

Gwen didn't reply. Winifred said, 'Yes dear.'

Gwen rounded on her and said irritably, 'Shut up Winifred, you don't know what you're talking about.'

'Yes dear.'

I should add that, despite Gwen's occasional outbursts of rudeness and irritability towards Winifred, she really cared for her very deeply. They had nursed together for over thirty-five years and when Winifred became seriously ill, it was mainly as a result of Gwen's aftercare that she survived. And even then it had its funny moments. I remember on one visit to Frenchay Hospital, when Winifred lay, rictus jawed and almost on her last gasp, Gwen, placing her hands firmly on her shoulders and, staring earnestly into her face threatened, 'If you die Winifred, I'll bloody kill you!'

She was too far gone even to say, 'Yes dear.'

There was another time, when Winfred was out of danger and convalescing in an old peoples' ward. She was by this time at the walking wounded stage. One of the old ladies lay flat on her back with her knees drawn up, legs spread wide apart and hands on her belly. 'Nurse, nurse,' she kept calling, 'My belly hurts.'

Winifred looked at her with some concern, then rushed over and said, '*Push* dear, *push*!'

By the time the others returned, clean and fresh from the swimming baths, we were all feeling quite cheerful and went off to a local restaurant where we all enjoyed a good meal and a couple of glasses of wine. All, that is, except Peggy, who had to make do with a bowl of soup. When we got back to the boat we were all oozing goodwill towards each other and went to bed feeling happy and relaxed.

TUESDAY

I woke up at 6.30am and, having now mastered the art of slithering from my bunk without disturbing the recumbent bodies below, I got up and after scrambling into my track suit, I left the boat and made my way to the public toilets to perform my morning ablutions. Then I bought some milk and a paper from the newsagents and sat on a park bench in the morning sunshine to read it. The previous evening I'd noticed a down-trodden, middle-aged woman walking about, wearing several layers of clothing, including a thick scarf and a woollen hat, which seemed a bit odd for high summer. She was pushing a large pram with the hood up, so I couldn't see if there was a baby inside. This morning I was surprised to see her lying fast asleep on a park bench near me, her pathetic belongings in the pram at her side, but thankfully, no baby. I was curious about her and wished she'd wake up so that I could engage her in conversation, but she slept on and I would never know what brought her to this sorry state.

When I got back to the boat everyone was up and breakfast was ready and I was the flavour of the morning for bringing back some milk. Over breakfast we discussed when, or what time we should leave Stratford. The others were all for staying another day and that would have been nice, but I calculated that if had taken us three and a half days to get here, it would take us that amount of time to get back, so we ought to start off pretty soon. Finally, we compromised by agreeing we would start back today but not until late afternoon. That settled, Peggy and Ross went off for another swim and Gwen, Winifred and I strolled up town and did some shopping.

We met up with the other two at Mistress Quickly's Café and speculated about the quaintness of the name and which Shakespearean play the character came from. Peggy said she thought it was The Merry Wives of Windsor. As the rest of us couldn't come up with an alternative, and because Peggy was more highly educated than the rest of us, I came down on her side, not actually having a clue. I checked when I got home and discovered she appears (in different roles) in four of his plays. How I wish I'd known that at the time.

Peggy and Ross showed us their purchases, which included sou'westers and shiny plastic waterproofs, and I showed them my new socks and plimsolls and sundry other bits and pieces. We did some grocery shopping on the way back to the boat and a collective feeling of goodwill broke out again.

When we eventually cast off at about 4pm, for no reason I could fathom, I began to feel nervous, although I did not communicate my feelings to the others. As it turned out, I had good reason to feel anxious, for the next five or six hours turned out to be the most alarming of the trip so far. We got safely out of the canal basin into a small, awkwardly angled lock, then under a low bridge without mishap and, not without a little regret, left Stratford and its enticing charms behind.

When Ross and Gwen left the boat and walked on to the next set of locks, I noticed that despite all the rain, the water was very low, so I steered to the centre of the canal to avoid getting stuck in the menacing banks of silt visible on either side. A boat coming towards us from the opposite direction had the same idea, but instead of gingerly easing past each other, it came on full with all of its four miles an hour power and forced me to the side where we went aground, leaving the other boat to chug merrily on its way. So there I was, boat stuck in the mud, heart stuck in my mouth and Peggy, white with terror and fury.

Once again, the people on the banks came to our rescue and, after pushing with poles, pulling with ropes, shouting, general panic and pandemonium, we were afloat again. I stared uneasily at the banks of silt and prayed we wouldn't meet another oncoming boat that would behave so selfishly. Thankfully, we didn't, but just as I was beginning to think our troubles were over we were faced with yet more problems.

A boat following us had failed to close the gates of the lock they had just left and when they reached our lock they had stupidly opened our lock gates whilst we were still in it. I tried to tell them they shouldn't have left the gates of the last lock open and *please* not to open our gates until we were out. They were young, strong, healthy looking chaps, who had probably hired the boat for a few hours and regarded us as a load of old fuddy-duddies. I called out to Ross and she ran back to the last lock to close the gates, roundly berating the crew of the offending boat as she went. I jumped off our boat and dashed back to the clueless crew to explain, again, that our gates must be kept closed until the lock had filled with water and then they could follow us through, but they didn't respond and we stared belligerently at each other. Another chap appeared from somewhere who spoke to me. It transpired they were foreigners but had one person on board who spoke English to whom I was able to explain about the gates.

By the time I got back to our boat, due to the water rushing out instead of in, it had dropped several feet and I had to jump from a great height to get back on board. My knees buckled as I landed and I banged my forehead on the wall of the lock, but I was in such a state of excitement, I hardly felt a thing.

Peggy, inside the boat with Winfred, popped a terrified head up and demanded,

'What the hell is going on and why have we been stuck in this lock for so long?'

We were now literally aground on the waterless floor of the lock, but with a confidence I was far from feeling I said, 'Don't worry Peg, we've got a bit of a water problem but it will soon be fixed.' I did not at that moment have a clue how, but, as in the past, a couple of men on the tow path saw the problem and ran to the next lock to open it to allow the water to flow down to us. I heaved a huge sigh of relief when we were finally afloat again and once more, thought our trials were over.

Not a bit of it. I'd just about got half way into the next lock before it too drained and I was stuck, half in and half out. Ross, being ahead, could not see the problem and kept yelling at me to keep coming forward.

'I can't move,' I yelled. 'I'm stuck again.'

'Use your throttle,' she screamed at me.

'I can't use the throttle when there's no water beneath me.'

More shouting, commanding, countermanding ensued with a few nasty expletives thrown in for good measure, before the doughty men on the tow path raced on to the next lock to open it. This time, as soon as I was out, I ignored the four mile an hour speed restrictions and raced ahead to the next lock as fast as the boat would go, to get inside before it, too drained.

At some point during all the mayhem, I managed to have a brief conversation with the English speaking man on the boat behind that had initially caused the problems and tried to explain what was happening. He was kind enough to enquire whether I'd hurt myself when I made my courageous leap onto the sunken boat. I told him I hadn't, but I was secretly pleased my brave act had actually been observed, even if they were only foreigners.

All locks now safely negotiated and the horrors of the last few hours behind us, we began to enjoy a pleasant, trouble free run. Peggy had recovered from her attack of the terrors and came to join me at the helm. Dear Peggy – I felt quite a rush of affection for her and I would always remember how gracious she had been when, all those years ago, I'd dashed her hopes of us sharing a life together, when she had given up so much to make it possible. But we had remained friends through thick and thin and now she was so frail and fearful, yet so brave, still striving to live life as normally as possible, yet knowing that there was little more that could be done for her.

It wasn't long before Gwen had reason to wail out her habitual cry: 'It's bloody raining again Winifred.'

'Yes dear.'

This was always said in an accusatory tone as if poor Winifred was personally responsible for the rain and was empowered to do something about it.

Because of all the traumas we didn't make the progress I thought necessary to get us back to Warwick on schedule, but we were all so tired we decided to moor up for the night at Wilmcote. We removed our soggy clothes, dried ourselves off and took stock of our various cuts and bruises. I was gratified when I looked in the mirror to see that the bump on my forehead was bruised and swollen. (It would have been disappointing if there'd been nothing to show for my trouble.) Ross had a swollen ankle, a blister on her heel and several minor bruises. It seemed a point of honour as to who'd got the most injuries and I think Gwen won by virtue of her busted thumb, the bang on her head from a barge pole and numerous scratches on arms and legs from the brambles. I noticed that the skin on the soles of my feet was all white, rubbery and wrinkled from standing in wet footwear for hours, but I didn't think that would count as an injury so I didn't mention it.

When we felt half decent again we left the boat and went to the Swan House Hotel for a meal, over which we re-lived the horror of the last few hours and felt a whole lot better for it.

Back on the boat I was prevented from sinking into the sleep I felt I so richly deserved as Peggy started snoring very loudly. Each time Ross told her to shut up she would mumble, 'I'm *not* snoring – only breathing deeply.' The deep breathing continued for a long time with Ross eventually adding her own 'deep breathing.'

WEDNESDAY

Ross and I got up early and by 7.30am we were ready to move off. We decided to go it alone leaving the others to rest as Peggy was feeling fragile, Gwen had a hangover and Winifred was her usual docile self.

Chugging peacefully along my thoughts turned to Gwen, who, despite her many paper qualifications, had no common sense at all and needed a 'blue print' for living. She also carried an outsize chip on her shoulder and was still convinced that nobody liked her (except Winifred, and she didn't count) despite my protestations to the contrary, although I acknowledged to myself that she didn't make it easy for people to love her. But she had taken a lot of flack, especially from Ross who, although essentially a caring person, could at times be quite overbearing and impervious to other people's opinions, especially when they differed from her own. Gwen, failing to realise this, would challenge and argue about everything and once or twice I thought they might even come to blows. Even so, I didn't think she deserved to be shouted down all the time and decided from now on to try and be extra kind to her.

Ross stayed at the helm with me and we had a good long run without any locks. The rain continued to pour down but by now we'd got used to it and it no longer mattered any more. We'd also learned to live with all the minor and major mishaps that had beset us from time to time, so it was par for the course that this brief spell of comparative tranquillity should be disturbed when Ross caught her heel on a metal ridge, stumbled and flew across the platform at me, disturbing my reverie and knocking me off my perch. She made a frantic grab for my knees as I was about to tumble backwards into the canal. I yelped and she looked stricken, but we quickly recovered from the shock and fell about laughing like fools. Ross was not usually given to unrestrained laughter as she took herself very seriously most of the time, so it was good that we could briefly bond in shared humour.

The others began to stir and Peggy cooked breakfast for us all. By the time we'd eaten it and were on our way again, the rain had stopped and the sun shone bright and warm, cheering us all up and making us feel well disposed towards each other.

It was our intention to travel as far as possible today, stamina and daylight permitting. However, when we reached the lock before the turning pool, which would take us back onto the Grand Union Canal, we once more became grounded in the lock and had to ease out again. It was explained to us by the nice friendly lock-keeper (the only one we'd seen) that because the Stratford Canal was not as well maintained as the Grand Union the water had drained out of the pool and it would be early next morning before it would fill up again, so they padlocked the lock gates and we had to stay put. Some knowledgeable people in other boats told us this was a common problem, as in some way beyond my comprehension, one canal often *stole* water from the other, but it would not be politic for me to mention here who allegedly stole from whom.

It was good to chat with some of the people queued up behind us and a consolation to know that many of the problems we'd encountered were not uncommon and not necessarily of our or anyone else's making. These things just happen, although we were obviously not sufficiently experienced or laid back to take it all in our stride. Despite everything, we were still well on target for getting back in time. After a wash and change of clothes we made our way to The Navigation Inn where we had a few drinks and nice chats with the locals, then back to the boat for a meal of lamb stew which had been left to cook whilst we were at the pub.

When we were getting ready for bed I examined my feet again. The rubbery soles were normal but my ankles were swollen from all the standing. Ross's feet were swollen from injury and all the walking she'd had to do. Gwen, surprisingly, complained of nothing.

I said to Ross, 'D'you realise you and Gwen have paid over a hundred pounds for the privilege of walking nearly all the way to Stratford and back, and the long way round at that.?'

She considered what I'd said for a moment, then exclaimed, 'We must be bloody mad!'

THURSDAY

As usual I woke up early, quietly slipped into my track suit without bothering to wash and walked along the towpath away from the waiting boats to find a secluded place to relieve myself – I still couldn't get used to the chemical toilet on board. When I got back I was pleased to see the pool had filled up and hoped we could get away before the other boat people were astir. I did not wish to be observed making an ass of myself trying to negotiate the tricky operation to take us back on ourselves into the Grand Union Canal. In the event, I needn't have worried as, following the lock keeper's instructions, I managed to execute an acute right turn and then a sharp left into the restricted turning area ready to go straight ahead for the next lock from whence we were homeward bound for Warwick. Although I say it myself, I thought I handled it all wonderfully well, especially as none of the others had yet bestirred themselves, although I could have wished that at least one of them had been on deck to hear the lockkeeper say admiringly, 'What a driver!'

At last the sun shone hot and strong and we had a delightful, trouble free run, with Peggy now confident enough to steer the boat alone, whilst the rest of us relaxed and I even found time to do a bit more filming. We were all feeling in good humour with ourselves and with each other, so much so that Gwen forgot all about the bullying she'd suffered, mostly at the hands of Ross, and said to her ingratiatingly, 'Your hair looks nice Ross.'

'It doesn't,' snapped Ross. 'It's a bloody mess just like everyone else's.'

I managed to film some of the wild flowers growing on the banks that hadn't been choked out of existence by the ever increasing proliferation of Himalayan Balsam. But there were some patches where the native wild flowers were still able to grow such as melilot, agrimony, musk mallow, monkey flower and wild marigold.

We reached the Hatton Flight of locks much more quickly than I expected and I hoped we might see our erstwhile knights of the canal Jim and Steve again. They said they would look out for us on our return, but then I realised it was early afternoon and they were probably still at work. I wanted to film our progress through the locks but Peggy was too scared to steer the boat through, so a man on one of the other boats volunteered to take over. He wasn't very good at it and banged the boat about so much against the sides of the lock walls that I feared for our safety and it was impossible to hold the camera steady, so I gave up the filming and went back to steering the boat and the man went back to rejoin his friends on the other boat.

After getting through the last of the locks Ross and Gwen said they were whacked and so was I. Peggy was surprisingly buoyant and Winifred was her usual complacent, compliant self. She'd given up on habitually repeating: 'Isn't it lovely – it's something I've always wanted to do,' but amused me at sometime during the trip by whispering confidentially, 'I think we'll try the Queen Mary next time dear.'

We reached an inviting spot that seemed a good place to take a break, so we moored up, had something to eat, then lay on the bank soaking up the sun. Ross and Peggy found some energy from somewhere and walked off to see if they could find a pub. They returned later bearing bottles of wine and bags of crisps and said they'd found out we were only about two miles away from Kate Boat Yard. We weren't due back until the following morning, so my calculations had gone wrong somewhere, although no one mentioned it.

A few glasses of wine later, we discussed whether to take the boat back a day early, or wait until the following morning. Peggy and Ross wanted to return it today. Gwen, who'd done the most complaining and was the most miserable throughout the trip, surprised us by saying she wanted to stay on the boat until the next day. Winifred, I knew would think whatever Gwen told her to think. I sat on the fence and kept my mouth shut.

'You want to stay on the boat until tomorrow don't you Winifred?' Gwen said, with the air of someone who knew the answer she wanted would be a mere formality.

I slyly winked at Winifred, who then infuriated Gwen by *not* saying 'Yes dear,' (her stock reply to every question) but, 'I'm not sure dear.'

Gwen rounded on her and shouted, 'You're so bland Winifred – so bloody bland.'

'Yes dear,' said Winifred, then after a few moments thought, added, 'but cornflower does have its uses.'

I put my weight behind the person that mattered most to me, so by a majority decision, the boat would be returned this day. Our next few hours cruising were quite the most pleasant of the whole trip, totally without incident and I was privately regretting our decision to take the boat back. But misfortune hadn't done with us yet and disaster struck once more. We were approaching the last lock on our journey and Ross, who was on the platform with me said she would manage it on her own, so I steered into the bank and she got off the boat. I was pulling away when Gwen, who had not been privy to the conversation, suddenly realised that Ross had left the boat and rushed to follow her. Before I had time to realise what was happening, she leapt off the boat, misjudging the distance and the limited extent of her athletic ability, missed the bank, plopped into the canal and disappeared beneath the murky waters.

'Oh my God! I yelled. 'Peggy come quick. Gwen's fallen in and she can't swim - and neither can I.'

I seized a boat hook for her to grab, whilst Peggy (who had certificates for life-saving) rushed up from the galley, kicked off her shoes and dived in after her. She surfaced, floundering and gasping and Peggy grabbed her and got her to the bank.

Ross, now alerted to the drama, came racing back and helped an exhausted Peggy back onto the boat, whilst I hauled Gwen on board. After we'd helped them out of their wet clothes, rubbed them down, found some dry clothing and made a cup of tea, they seemed little the worse for the experience.

However, Ross couldn't help having a go at Gwen for being so stupid as to fall in. Then she had a go at Peggy (given her state of health) for jumping in to rescue her, and me for not throwing a life belt in (never mind that I don't think we actually had one). I think she was secretly miffed that she'd missed the opportunity of being the heroine of the hour, but we took her ranting in good part, so relieved were we that the incident hadn't ended in real tragedy.

There was now no question of staying another night and we arrived back at Kate Boat Yard about 5.30pm. The proprietor didn't seem a bit surprised to see us, so perhaps they were used to people coming back early. I didn't kick the boat as we got off, for now, in a perverse sort of way, I had become oddly attached to it, although I wasn't going to admit this to the others.

All safely back at my home in Leamington Spa, after a proper bath and change into some decent clothing, we sat down to watch the film I'd made of our adventure. We watched a boat serenely chugging towards us, the top of which was colourfully be-decked with pots of summer bedding plants, with an elderly, weather bronzed man at the helm placidly sucking on a curve handled pipe. We marvelled at the incredibly beautiful scenery. All seemed unbelievably idyllic and tranquil, with only the singing of the birds, the gentle lap of water against the side of the boat and the soothing purr of the engine to disturb the silence and enhance the sense of perfect peace. I hadn't noticed the scenery, or heard a bird sing, or noticed the engine purring

217

soothingly whilst we were on the boat and neither had the others, and anyone watching the film would find it hard to believe all the fears, toil, sweat and swearing that had gone into the making of all this seeming tranquillity.

Warm, clean and comfortable, with a few more glasses of wine inside us, we were now all in remarkably high spirits and able to laugh at all the drama of the week. We were also amazed and gratified to see our weather tanned, healthy looking faces, despite it having rained most of the time. However, Ross threatened to throttle Gwen when she seriously suggested we book another canal holiday for the following year.

I think the real benefit of this holiday for me was the discovery of how helpful strangers can be and the realisation that the age of chivalry is not dead, especially when it is altruistically extended to a gaggle of old ladies.

Chapter 54

Departed Friends.

A few months after the canal holiday Gwen died suddenly of a heart attack. Winifred went into a care home and died shortly after and Peggy's cancer reared it's ugly head once more. She didn't want to stay in Brighton after her retirement and when I retired she and Ross decided to move to the Midlands, and bought a bungalow in Warwick, about a mile from where I lived. My friend John left his job as a progress chaser in a Coventry factory and moved to Brighton to live in Peggy's house. She made him responsible for collecting the rents from the other tenants and he was also made manager of Ross's night club, where he came into his element and drunk himself and the profits into oblivion.

Now that I was retired, much of the time I'd hoped to spend pursuing my own hobbies and interests was severely curtailed by the obligation imposed on me in helping Ross look after Peggy. It wasn't something I did with a glad heart; in fact at times I found it quite irksome, but I would never have shown it by a word or a look. It wasn't easy, what with the worry of Peggy's deteriorating health and Ross's ever increasing alcohol dependency. When she'd had too much to drink she either became embarrassingly mawkish or fiendishly quarrelsome, and it was sometimes difficult to decide which was the worse. Despite all, I would always feel a sense of gratitude towards her for coming into Peggy's life, thereby easing my perennial sense of guilt, and if this was the price I had to pay – then so be it.

On 1st September 1994 Peggy died. She'd been in a coma for two days, not moving a limb or a muscle; then surprisingly, on the third day she briefly recovered consciousness. All the agony and fear seemed to have melted away and she lay with an almost beatific smile playing round the corners of her mouth.

'All right Peg?' I said quietly. She feebly raised her thumb to indicate all was well.

Her lips were parched and dry and I leant over and moistened them with a wet tissue.

With her last breath she whispered, almost inaudibly, 'I love you Lynn.'

'I love you too Peg,' I whispered back and hoped she'd heard me before she drifted off into the hereafter.

Chapter 55

Net Curtains

Now that I was more free, Muriel and I went on a few coaching holidays together, a highly recommended way of spending a holiday when one is in ones declining years. For most of the time we got along very well together, that is, just so long as I refrained from challenging her in her rightness about everything. She would sometimes say, half jokingly, 'I am not a difficult or argumentative person – what I say is right and that's it!' She also had a disconcerting tendency to do a subject to death without having the sensitivity to realise that the subject might not be as riveting to the hapless listener as it was to herself. The only thing that made it bearable was that she didn't expect an intelligent response – just a willing ear and the occasional trite comment. I remember the last holiday we had together when we went to the Lake District. We were lucky enough to have a seat immediately behind the coach driver, so had an unfettered view of everything.

We got on our coach in Coventry and shortly into the journey she told me she'd bought some new net curtains.

'Oh nice,' I said.

Our first stop was Nuneaton and Muriel, who was looking out of the window remarked:

'Ooh, look at *those* pretty net curtains, aren't they lovely?'

'Oh, yeah,' I said, briefly glancing.

We travelled on, the driver pointing out places of interest on the way and our next stop was Lichfield.

'I don't like *those* net curtains much,' she said, pointing to another house which had caught her attention.

Without bothering to look, I said, 'Why, what's wrong with them?'

'They're a horrible dirty grey and look as if they could do with a good wash,' she said, then added severely, 'can't you see?'

I gave a swift glance in the direction indicated. 'Yeah, they are a bit dirty I suppose.'

'A *bit* dirty,' she blurted, much affronted. 'They're filthy!'

We continued our journey and the driver continued to point out places of historical interest, about which Muriel seemed to know a lot more than he, and would, from time, feed me the additional facts, which I *did* find interesting.

Stafford was our next pick-up point and she fixed her sight on yet another house.

'Now I like *those* nets,' she said, 'don't you?'

'Which ones are you looking at?'

'*Those,*' she said, pointing. 'The cream ones that are all nicely scalloped.'

'Oh yeah – nice.'

We stopped at some traffic lights and a high rise block of flats to our left caught her attention.

'Well,' she said, 'you wouldn't be able to see whether the people living up there had nice nets or not, would you?'

'No, I s'pose not really.'

'Do you know,' she continued, 'I once went to Downing Street on a demonstration and was shocked to see the net curtains at Number 10 looked ever so crumpled and uncared for.'

'Never!'

'They *were* – I couldn't believe it!'

'I bet you couldn't,' I replied, delving into the depths of my being to try and find some enthusiasm for the shameful state of Number 10's nets.

In my resolve to be as pleasant and uncontroversial as I knew how, I refrained from telling her that I found the subject of net curtains terminally boring, but as we were now speeding along the motorway with no houses to look at, the subject died a merciful death.

We reached Lancaster and the driver drew our attention to an unusual looking house with rounded, castellated walls, incongruously built in red brick and standing at the end of a row of very ordinary, conventional looking houses.

We eagerly craned our necks forward the better to see. He told us to look up at the top window on the left. We screwed our necks, raised our eyes and eagerly inclined our ears to receive yet another snippet of historical interest.

'You see those net curtains,' he said. 'We've got some just like that at home.'

'Fancy that!' said Muriel.

I smiled a secret smile.

Chapter 56

A New Life and Life's End.

Shortly after Peggy had died, Clare's husband – Jonathan - had also died from cancer. I stayed in Leamington for a few more years, but as I now had more friends in Wales, and what relations I had, save one, had now moved to Wales, it seemed the right time for me to move. There was no longer anything to keep me rooted in Leamington, so at the ripe old age of seventy-four, I upped sticks and re-located to Hay-on-Wye. A friend who was a writer invited me to join the Hay Writers' Circle, which added a new dimension to my life, having harboured, from a child, a secret ambition to be a writer, but never believed I had the education or skill to make this a reality. I've since had several articles accepted for publication and acted as chairman of the Hay Writers' for over ten years until retiring at the age of ninety. During this time I also had, along with other members of the group, the opportunity to read some of my work at the Hay Festival of Literature. It may be thought that in my mid seventies it was a bit late to start a new avocation, but I took heart from a quotation by George Eliot who said: It's never too late to be – what you might have been."

Joe and Muriel drove from Kent to come and stay with me in my new abode and although I didn't need it, I was glad she put her stamp of approval on my new move. She liked to act the older sister at times, and although she was actually six years my junior, I was happy to go along with her feeling of superiority. After all, she *was* the married one with a family and that gave her an imagined state of supremacy over me. In any event, she could always complete the newspaper crosswords much more quickly than I and that in itself was no mean feat and something for which I could admire her. It was a very happy visit but in the event, it turned out to be her last.

It was the beginning of November 1998 when I had a telephone call from her to say she was back from her holiday on the Isle of Wight.

'Oh good,' I said, 'and did you enjoy it?'

'Well, yes,' she said hesitantly, 'but I was *so* tired all the time. I hardly knew how to put one foot in front of the other.'

I made sympathetic noises and said I knew exactly how she felt and hoped she'd feel better soon. A few days later she phoned me again, this time to say she was in the Medway Hospital.

'What are you doing there?' I asked.

'They're doing tests,' she said, 'but they won't know what's wrong until they get the results.'

I drove to the hospital a few days later and went straight to the ward. It wasn't visiting time, but when I told the nurse I'd come all the way from Wales and could she let me see my sister, she led me into the single ward and said, 'You've got a visitor from Wales to see you.

'Good, it will be Susan,' she said.

'No love. It's me, but I think Susan will be along later.'

'Oh, *you*.' she said.

I was sorry to disappoint her and shocked to see how dreadfully ill she looked. The date was significant because she thought it was Remembrance Sunday (which it wasn't) and indicated she wanted to watch the memorial service on the T.V. It was something we both did every year, catching our throats at the sight of the elderly, frail ex-service men and women bravely marching along to the compelling beat of the military bands; then spilling the odd tear when they played the sweetly sorrowing strains of Walford Davies' Solemn Melody and Elgar's Nimrod variations, and we always joined in the singing *O Valiant Hearts*. It's strange how one can, in some perverse way, actually enjoy being sad, provided, that is, the sadness is not too personal.

Muriel was in no state to be argued with, so I put some money in the slot and switched on the television hanging over the bed. I inclined the T.V. this way and that and asked her what she could see.

'Bugger all,' she said.

I was surprised because, unlike me, she seldom if ever swore. It was ironic that these were the last coherent words she spoke. Susan arrived later that night and Muriel was sufficiently compos mentis to realise that she was there, even if she was beyond speech.

We stayed with her until late evening when she began to snore loudly. I looked at Sue and said, 'I think she's sleeping now. Shall we go?'

The hospital phoned at five o'clock the following morning to say she had died.'

Chapter 57

Chance Encounters

Sheerness Station on the Isle of Sheppey must be one of the most dreary railway stations in the land at the best of times, but on this damp, gloomy day in November it seemed more gloomy and scruffy than ever.

Standing around in the dirty, unwelcoming waiting area, I consoled myself with the thought that I would only be here for ten minutes at the most before speeding my way homewards. The ten minutes were up and no train arrived. Presently the ticket clerk emerged and announced that the 9.50 train to London had been cancelled, but added that a bus would be along in about forty minutes to take us to Sittingbourne, from where we could catch a later train to London.

I glanced around at the other passengers, some of whom were huffing and grumbling about the vagaries and inadequacies of the railway service, whilst others continued to chat happily. Apart from the dedicated readers of newspapers, most of the people seemed to have at least one companion with whom to while away the waiting and I felt old, lonely and out of place. So I was pleased when two pleasant women standing near spoke to me and enquired, 'You got far to go love?'

'Yes,' I replied, adding, 'I'm getting a bit anxious though in case I miss my coach connection at Victoria.'

They showed concern and in a pronounced Kent accent said, 'You don't come from round 'ere do you.'

'No', I replied. 'I live on the Welsh borders but I came here to attend my sister's funeral.'

'Oh,' said the older of the two ladies, 'what she die of then?'

'Leukaemia,' I said, and glad of someone to talk to added, 'She only lived for a few days after being diagnosed. She told me she'd been to her doctor but he told her to stop wasting his time and come back when she was due for her three monthly check-up. But her husband was so worried he took her to the Medway Hospital where she was admitted straight away.'

'Cor, ain't that bleeding typical!' exploded the younger woman. 'Who was 'er doctor then?'

I mentioned his name.

'Oh 'im,' they chorused. 'He used to be one of the doctors at our practice but they got rid of him because he was bleeding useless. He wants reporting.'

'Yes,' I murmured, without the slightest intention of doing any such thing. But I was curiously comforted by the fact that two total strangers could be so outraged on my behalf and I felt a rush of gratitude towards them.

I began to feel a bit tearful and to hide my embarrassment and possibly theirs, I moved away on the pretext of finding somewhere to sit. I spotted a seat in the far corner and made for it, dragging my wheeled suit case behind me and accidentally nudged a pushchair. I turned to apologise to the young woman in charge of it, who gave me a filthy look whilst attending to the lighting of her cigarette, with total disregard for the sign which said: NO SMOKING.

I sat down, furtively dabbed my eyes, then focussed my attention on the young mother, not so much because she was smoking, but because of her arresting appearance, which was obviously calculated to make people notice her. She had a nice figure, if a bit too thin, and might have been pretty were it not for her assiduous efforts to make herself look otherwise. Her hair was jet black, short, gelled and spiked. Her skin was translucently white, made to look the more so by the liberally applied black eye-liner, purplish brown eye-shadow, black eye-brow pencil and mascara, and purple lipstick. She seemed self-assured and obviously comfortable with her image and indeed, why shouldn't she be? It was just that, in the sleepy little Welsh border town where I live everyone looks so ordinary.

Shifting my gaze from mother to baby, I was surprised to see it looked quite cherubic, with fat pink cheeks and fair curling hair. The child began to grizzle and to quieten it, the mother took a Swiss Roll from her bag and from behind the pushchair, stuffed a lump into the baby's mouth with one hand, the while she smoked with the other.

Her hard-eyed male companion, whose features were equally arresting, festooned as they were, with safety pins in his eyebrows and bits of metal dangling from his ears, lips and nostrils, appeared with plastic cups of hot drinks. She wordlessly accepted the proffered cup, took a sip, then to my alarm, carelessly placed the cup on the hood of the pushchair in order to stuff more cake into the fractious baby's mouth. The husband glanced in my direction and caught me staring and to cover my unease I gave him a nervous, half smile. He advanced towards me, stooped and said, 'Can I get you something to drink love?'

'No thank you,' I said, 'but it's kind of you to ask,' then added, 'What a beautiful baby you have, so lovely I couldn't keep my eyes off it.' As I looked into his face, all the bits of dangling metal which festooned it, suddenly disappeared and all I saw was the hard dark eyes soften to brown velvet. I looked across at his wife and smiled – she smiled back – which just goes to show. I was also relieved to see she'd finished her hot drink before it accidentally fell off the pushchair hood and scalded the baby.

I turned my attention elsewhere and two young men now became the focus of my interest. They seemed an unlikely pairing, the one being short, stocky, uncommunicative and dour looking. He wore an anorak that appeared a couple of sizes too big; tatty jeans that were too long and concertina-ed over a badly worn pair of trainers.

He was perched on top of the back rest of a plastic bench with his feet resting where his bottom should have been. His head was bent forward and in his hands was a half size bottle of Napoleon brandy, which, when he wasn't sipping from it, he lovingly caressed, occasionally pressing the neck of the bottle to his lips with as much reverence as if it were a sacred rosary.

His mate was tall, lithe and slim, with a pale, mischievous face. He was not clothed to protect himself from the prevailing weather, wearing only a thin pair of blue jeans, topped with a white, short-sleeved T-shirt. He kept on the move, cheerfully nodding and winking at anyone who caught his eye. He had a half size bottle of whisky from which he too, took regular slugs.

A large, see-through plastic wallet rested upright on the bench at the feet of the dour one in which I could discern two razors, an assortment of paper documents and several business cards, which served to fuel further my speculation as to what these two men had in common. I shamelessly tried to listen to snippets of conversation that passed between them and was able to establish that the dour one had a Scottish accent and the lively one sounded like a Londoner.

I heard the dour one say: 'Try this one Col,' as he removed a card from the plastic wallet and handed it over.

Col scuttled off to a telephone kiosk and returned shortly.

He tore the card in two, dropped it on the floor, then reported: 'That's no good Dunk, it's only an answering phone.'

Another card was extracted. Col left and returned. 'Any good?' enquired Dunk.

'Nah, there's no reply.'

Another card was handed over and this time Col returned all smiles. 'Bingo! I've made an appointment for us to see this geezer in Bromley at three o'clock.'

A flicker if interest crossed the features of Dunk as he gave a curt nod, then they both swigged copiously from their respective bottles. It obviously wasn't a close relationship that threw these two men together and yet there was an indefinable bond – why else would they have their pathetic possessions in the same container. Perhaps they were left-over spectators from an important football match, but this thought was quickly dismissed when I remembered they don't have important football matches on the Isle of Sheppey. Holiday makers perhaps? Hardly, in the middle of November. Although shabbily dressed, they looked too clean and healthy to be dossers or derelicts and I continued to speculate about them.

My reverie was interrupted by the announcement that the bus had arrived.

The two ladies who'd spoken with me previously called out, 'You all *wight* love?'

'Yes thank you,' I smiled, and was about to speak further when Col sidled up and said, 'Can I carry your case love?'

'Thank you, most kind.'

'Got far to go?'

'Well yes,' I said. 'I'm going to London Victoria, then I'm catching a coach to Wales.'

His face lit up. 'Me *Muvver* was born in Wales.'

'Oh, whereabouts?' I asked.

'Pontypool. D'you know it?'

'Yes,' I lied, for I did not want to disappoint him.

Emboldened by his willingness to make conversation, I seized the moment to satisfy my curiosity. 'Have you and your friend been holidaying on the Island?'

'Well, you could say that,' he replied, 'but it was a long one at Her Majesty's expense.'

It was only then that I remembered there was an open prison on the Isle of Sheppey and he and his mate must have been released that morning. Hence, I suppose, the celebratory half bottles of booze and the shared plastic container.

'Oh really,' I said with a questioning look.

'Not for *nuffink* bad,' he said reassuringly. 'It's just that I've got this terrible memory, especially when I go into shops.'

'Oh, right,' I said, slightly amused at his euphemism for thieving.

He politely stood to one side and helped me and other lady passengers on to the bus, before briefly disappearing. Oh Lord, I thought for one panic stricken moment: I hope he remembers it's MY suitcase he's carrying. I needn't have worried. He'd taken my case to be placed in the bowels of the bus and reappeared, all nods and winks and smiles as he made his way down the length of the coach to sit by his mate Dunk.

I sat, idly gazing out of the bus window, reflecting how interesting strangers are and, despite appearances to the contrary, how kind and friendly they can be.

Chapter 58

Child Minding

A few days after I got home I looked through the few relics I'd rescued from Muriel's desk. A family friend picked up some exercise books that were filled with Muriel's handwriting and asked me if I'd read them. I hadn't and he told me that I should, saying he'd read them and they were "ever so interesting." I put them to one side, intending to look at them at some future date. There were a few photographs which I thought I'd like to keep and there was also a letter.

When I saw my writing on the envelope I said to her husband, 'Good Lord Joe, there's a letter here from me.'

'Oh yes,' he said. 'She kept all your letters.'

'*Did* she?' I said, 'Where are the others then?'

'I threw them out with the rest of the rubbish – must have missed that one.'

Muriel and I often wrote long letters to each other and I was sorry I hadn't kept any of hers. I took the letter and consigned it to the same drawer as the hand-written manuscript on her life up until her first marriage, until one day, looking for something else, I came across them. The letter was written when I was doing a stint of child minding for my niece (her now divorced daughter) Susan, whilst she was away on a business trip:

15th March 1994

My dear Muriel,

I'm on the last leg of my child minding stint and am, surprisingly, still sane – but only just - having managed, with considerable restraint, to resist death by strangulation of the children.

When I arrived last Friday I was told Katie would be having a few friends round on Saturday evening and that I would be taking Tim to the cinema so we'd be out of the way for the party, and when we got back it would be time for the 'friends' to leave. I asked where I was supposed to be taking Tim to the cinema and was told it was in Swansea.

'Oh no!' I protested. 'At my age there is no way I'm prepared to wander around a strange city at night for anyone.' So that was that.

Saturday morning and early evening flew by as I raced around fulfilling all the instructions Sue had given me viz: 1. Go to Builder's Merchant and pay for wood that had been ordered and arrange for delivery. 2. Buy victorian taps for kitchen sink. 3. Arrange delivery of kitchen surfaces. 4. Get Katie's audition tape de-vocalised. 5. Arrange for Jason to come and build kitchen. 6. Contact plumber. 7. Arrange delivery of kitchen flooring. 8. Pick up video of The King and I (in which Tim plays the part of Anna's son.)

What little time was left to me I spent filling in the large cracks between skirting and wall on the stairs and wherever else I could reach. There is an infestation of bluebottle flies here, which is not to be wondered at given the number of holes in the plaster in which they must have over-wintered. I have squirted fly spray in all reachable orifices and now the flies are noisily buzzing around in a frenzied dance of death.

Even if I had agreed to take Tim to the cinema, I certainly now had no energy for it, so when it was time for Katie's party I took him upstairs where we sat on the bed and played cards and chequers, at which he beat me every time. To be outwitted by a ten year old is quite disconcerting, but he was pleased. At 9 o'clock he went to bed with the cat (of which I strongly disapproved) and I waited patiently upstairs until eleven o'clock, when I went down to call time on the revellers. Katie asked if two of the boys could stay as they'd missed their last bus home, had no money for a taxi and when I suggested they could walk home, I was told it was pouring with rain. With reluctance, I gave my permission for them to stay, then spent a sleepless night worrying about it.

Got up at 7 am and came downstairs to find not two but four boys and a girl sprawled over the living room floor and empty bottles and beer cans strewn everywhere. Furious, I unceremoniously booted them all out, but not before letting them know exactly what I thought of them and the disgusting mess they'd made. A mad scramble ensued. The empties and the over-nighters disappeared as if by magic and Katie, unbidden, leapt into action with the vac – which actually works, though little else here seems to.

I went into the kitchen to make a drink and opened a tin marked 'Tea' only to find that one of last night's mindless morons had tipped cat food pellets into it, plus gravy granules and the remains of a packet of salt. An egg had been broken on the newly fitted kitchen floor and left where it was. I screamed at Katie to come and clear it up, which she did after a fashion, then I discovered several cigarette burns, spilled drinks and another broken egg on the new living room carpet. I freaked out, lost the plot and all Katie could say was, 'Calm down Auntie, you'll give yourself a heart attack!'

I didn't have a heart attack, but continued to rant like a raving lunatic, the while I did my best to clear up the mess. I sent Katie to the shop to buy some tea, coffee milk et cetera and when she'd gone I sat down and wept with fury. I tried to punish Katie by telling her she was 'grounded' for the rest of the day, but it wasn't much of a punishment anyway, as she seemed to spend much of the time on the telephone telling friends she was 'grounded' as if she'd been given a reward for doing something terribly clever or worthy.

When I could bear it no longer, I screeched at her, 'Katie! Will you get off that telephone and help me clear this house up.'

Once again I was met with the same infuriating response: 'Chill out Auntie, you'll give yourself a heart attack.' A red mist descended, I charged towards her intent on murder, tripped over the bloody cat and went sprawling at her feet.

'Must go!' she shouted into the mouth piece. 'I think auntie's having a seizure.'

You'll be relieved to know I didn't actually have a 'seizure' and neither did I kill Katie. By mid-afternoon I was more-or-less restored to my rightful mind; peace reigned and because I was too tired to do battle with the half finished kitchen I rescinded Katie's 'grounding' and took them out for a meal at a local café. Katie, I have to confess, became really helpful about the house and solicitous towards me, unaware, of course, of my erstwhile evil intentions towards her.

I asked Tim if his school clothes were organised for Monday morning. He assured me they were and I was, frankly, too weary to drag myself upstairs to check. Imagine my horror when he came down to breakfast wearing an old grey shirt busting at the buttons and odd socks. I found a clean white shirt that fitted, but searched in vain for two matching socks.

Katie got up late, despite my having called her several times. She erupted out of the front door with me calling after her, 'You haven't had your breakfast!' I raced after her with a piece of toast smothered in peanut butter, which she snatched from my grasp as if it was a relay baton, and flew on her way.

Jason continued with the work he had to do on the kitchen; the plumber arrived and did what he had to do, and the de-vocalised tape of Puccini's O Mio Babbino Caro was delivered in time for Katie to sing to it for her audition for entry to the Welsh College of Music and Drama. Having failed on Saturday, I have now succeeded in getting the video of the Melyncrythan Amateur Operatic Society performing The King and I. I also bought a pack of six socks (all the same colour) for Tim, so things are coming together and I'm beginning to feel quite benignant. Must stop now to get the evening meal prepared.

Not very popular with Tim at the moment. When he got home from school, despite my cheery greeting, he looked a bit sullen.

'You don't look very happy,' I said. 'Is everything okay?'

'No,' he said. 'I haven't had a drink all day.'

'And whose fault is that?' I said testily. 'I packed you a bottle of orange juice didn't I?'

'It's not orange juice,' he said, 'it's cough mixture.'

Made a mental note to wear my glasses when packing lunch box in future and told him to get himself a glass of proper orange juice then do his homework. At this point he suddenly remembered his Bambi video was overdue at the library, so we set off to return it and I was annoyed to have to pay a late return fine.

Arrived home to find Katie in a panic. 'Where have you been?' she demanded. 'I'll be late for my guitar lesson.' So it was off in the car again to deliver her to her lesson.

More cajoling of Tim to do his homework to no avail, so thought I would shame him into making a start by saying I'd do it myself. 'Thanks Auntie,' he said.

Just about to start getting evening meal when the phone rang. It was Katie wanting me to pick her up from her guitar lessen. Is there no end to it!

The cat became a bit of an issue as I was quite adamant that I didn't want it in the bedrooms. Do what they like when I'm gone but not whilst I'm in charge. So you can imagine I was none too pleased when, shortly after getting into bed, the cat started meowing very loudly. I shot out of bed yelling, 'Get that damned cat out of my bedroom!' Katie and Tim came rushing in laughing and falling about like fools. There was no cat. They'd recorded it meowing earlier and put the recorder under my bed. God knows what they'd done to the poor thing to make it meow so long and loud.

As I recall, apart from Jason accidentally blocking a gas pipe whilst doing things in the kitchen, and then losing a whole days work because his wife dropped him off and cleared off to work with all his tools still in the car and the plumber switching the water off when he came back to do a minor adjustment to the taps and forgetting to switch it on again, the rest of the week went reasonably peacefully. Katie was pleased that she'd passed her audition and we really enjoyed watching Tim in the video of The King and I.

Sue arrived home last night after a successful business trip to Harrogate with a book full of orders for her bridal gowns including a big order from Harrods. I'm now off to Neath to meet her for lunch, after which I shall wing my way back to Leamington to the peace and solitude I feel I now so richly deserve.

Much love,

Lynn xx

Joe grieved heavily over the death of Muriel and now, no longer under her restraining influence, he indulged his sorrow by freely imbibing huge amounts of alcohol. He died twelve months after her of a liver complaint and his ashes were planted in the back garden next to Muriel's beneath the rose arbour. They both loved their garden and it seemed an appropriate thing to do at the time, but now I'm not so sure. Chris, who was now living alone in the house, eventually sold it and moved to Wales to be nearer the rest of the family, so we have no place of remembrance to visit.

The new owners of the property will doubtless be unaware of what might be fertilising the roses.

.

Chapter 59

Cracking Up.

I was now in my late seventies and although I'd always been a pretty healthy person, inevitably, I began to develop a few age related health problems. I was short of breath and energy and walking more than a few yards was becoming a bit of a problem, and I would think: This is what it's like being old – live with it. And as my painfully honest nephew -Christopher said to me, 'After all, people of your age are not only cracking up – they're usually decomposing.'

It was a great comfort to be to know that I'd still got all my marbles and I didn't seriously think that I was actually decomposing. I coped with extreme tiredness as best I could until one day when I woke up feeling more energised than I had done for ages, and thought it would be a good time to catch up with the housework that had for so long been neglected. First I put the dirty breakfast dishes into the sink to join those left there from the night before, then rolled up my sleeves to do battle with the washing up. A shaft of sunlight came streaming through the kitchen window, showing up the dust and high-lighting a few cobwebs webs hanging from the ceiling. I abandoned the sink, hauled out the vacuum cleaner and sucked up the cobwebs, then carefully re-arranged the dust that had peacefully settled everywhere. I then went through the whole house, dusting, polishing and vacuuming. All done, I staggered from room to room, congratulating myself on my nice clean house and wondered how I could have neglected it for so long.

Before I could accomplish all the tasks I'd set myself, such as the washing up and perhaps a bit of gardening, I began to tire, so flopped down for a rest. At this point I recalled a conversation I'd once had with a very Welsh old lady whilst sitting on a bench in a shopping precinct.

I said, 'Isn't it nice to have a bench to sit on whilst waiting for someone.'

'Yes,' she said. 'I don't know how I'd manage without it. When I'm at home, I do *do* bit, then I do have to sit a bit. Then I do *do* a bit more and I do have to sit a bit more.' I knew exactly what she meant.

So I sat a bit, then made myself a light lunch, but was too tired to eat it so threw it our for the birds and went back to the kitchen sink to have another go at the washing up. But I couldn't face it, so returned to the living room and flopped into the reclining chair, my heart pounding like a sledge hammer.

This is it, I thought. This is what it feels like when you are dying, and I lay back in the recliner to await, what I hoped, would be a pain free passage into oblivion. Lying there, it occurred to me that I hadn't made a Will. Too late now. I hadn't got much to leave anyway, so I dismissed the thought and reverted to dying mode. I considered ringing my friend Clare to come to my aid but decided against it – I would feel such an absolute fool if I didn't die after all. However, I did struggle to my feet again to unlock the front door – just in case I died and no one could get in. I crab-walked my way back to the recliner, where I sank down once more to expire.

I felt pleased (if one could feel pleased when one is about to die) that at least the house was in good order. Then I remembered the unwashed dishes, so I arose again and made my way to the kitchen to perform, what I believed would be my last task on earth. This time I managed to finish the job before dragging myself back to the living room, where, pandering to my innate sense of drama, I decided to make an entry in my diary recording my last moments.

So I wrote, in a spidery, unsteady hand: *Feeling strange and very unwell. Insurance details in brown quarto envelope, second drawer down. Writing is difficult. Time 4pm.*

As a final act, I put on a C.D. of Faure's Requiem; arranged myself decently in the reclining chair, then lay back once more to die, gracefully and beautifully, drifting off to the moving strains of *In Paradisum*. I didn't know how long I'd been dead before I started knocking on the door of Heaven. No answer, so I knocked again and woke myself up. It was *my* door being knocked. I struggled out of my comatose state and went to answer it.

There stood a personable young man with an attractive lady by his side. They introduced themselves, mentioned the religious denomination to which they belonged and asked me if I believed in God.

Just to be on the safe side, I mumbled, 'Yes. Yes I do. Has he sent you to get me?'

They looked a bit startled and took a few paces backwards.

'Oh, I'm sorry,' I said. 'I'm not dead after all.'

They shoved a few pamphlets at me and hastened away, leaving me smiling vacuously at their retreating backs.

It was shortly after this that I went to the surgery for the standard annual blood test given to pensioners of a certain age as a matter of course. It revealed that my haemoglobin count was dangerously low and I was whisked off to hospital for a blood transfusion. After further tests, I was strung up to a machine whilst blood slowly dripped into me throughout the night and although I hardly slept a wink, I couldn't believe how invigorated I felt afterwards. It was just as if I'd been born again. My G.P. told me later that my blood count was so low, it was a wonder I was able to get out of bed, never mind continue to function. What a debt I owe to the truly altruistic people who give blood anonymously to save the lives of anonymous people.

Chapter 60

Glider Flight

I met and made a lot of friends during my time in the Writers' Circle, many of whom are now dead, others in care homes and some still very much alive. Joan, not only a writer but also a well known artist and now in her nineties, reminisced about the good times we'd had together when she was still mobile and up for a bit of adventure. One of her more notable escapades was when she was rapidly approaching her 87th birthday and, being of a feisty nature, wanted to do something different and daring to celebrate it. What was more, she was anxious for me (only two years her junior) to join her in whatever bizarre escapade she might dream up and which, knowing her as I do, left me in no doubt that whatever it was, it would not be suitable for two very elderly ladies.

Ever since I'd known her, Joan tended to be accident prone, so I tried to think of something really daring, like a bungee jump from a great height, or abseiling down a huge cliff, or even hang gliding, plus a few more ridiculous ideas in the hope that she would give up on her fanciful whim.

But Joan doesn't give up easily and she called me one day, brimming with enthusiasm, and said, 'I've had a good idea.'

'Yes…' I said cautiously, 'and what's that?'

'You know you mentioned hang-gliding. Well, we can do the next best thing. I've been in touch with the Talgarth Glider Club and booked a flying lesson for us both.'

The flight was to take place on her birthday, Saturday 14th July and short of developing a serious illness or breaking a leg, I could see no way of backing out without being thought a wimp.

The big day arrived and we set off accompanied by Clare, armed with her cine camera, to record the event for posterity.

We arrived about 9.30am and hung about the airfield for hours waiting for the wind to drop and the clouds to clear, so that conditions would be more favourable. Although I would never have admitted it, I secretly hoped the weather would *not* change and I would be spared the alarming prospect of taking to the skies in a flimsy, engine-less contraption.

Our flight had been booked for 10am and it said something for Joan's determination and my patience that we were still there at four o'clock in the afternoon, when it was at last deemed safe to take off.

All fury spent, the wind had transformed itself into a gentle, uplifting breeze, which parted the clouds and allowed the sun to burst through, revealing a cerulean, high summer sky. I urged Joan to go up first and Clare and I watched, with some amusement, as the instructor placed a heavy parachute on her back, which made her legs buckle. She was supposed to bend forward and grab the straps dangling from the back and bring them forward through her legs and secure them at the front. But due to the weight of the parachute, her small stature and totally un-athletic little body, she wasn't able to accomplish this.

The instructor observed her for a few moments trying to think of a way round the problem. Then he smiled and mischievously enquired, 'Permission to grope Ma'am?' Whereupon he thrust his hands between her legs, yanked the straps through and duly secured them.

The next difficulty was getting into the narrow cockpit of the glider. No steps, no doors. Entry was gained by lifting the hinged cockpit cover and climbing in as best one could, and after much heaving and hauling Joan finally plopped hard into the front seat. The instructor climbed into the seat behind and they were away, dragged off the airfield by an ancient light aircraft which eventually catapulted the glider into the blue yonder.

We watched until they were out of sight and half an hour or more later they were back, elegantly floating down to a perfect landing. Joan was hauled out of the cockpit, looking quite pale, and advanced towards us on wobbly legs.

'Did you enjoy it Joan?' I asked, with some apprehension.

'Not much,' she grinned sheepishly, 'but I'm glad I did it.'

Now it was my turn. Happily, I was spared the indignity of having to be "groped" and was able to reach the straps to fasten the parachute and take my place in the cockpit with little ado. But I was not much cheered when the instructor said that putting on the parachute was a mere formality – if we had to bale out there would not be time for it to open before we hit the ground.

'What a comforting thought,' I said, with a tinge of sarcasm.

A frisson of fear short through me as we hurtled along the flat stretch of grass, lifted off and became airborne, then, with an alarming thwack, finally became detached from our powered aircraft. But my fear was soon dispelled, so absorbed was I in listening to the instructions of the pilot, who was seated behind me and had an identical set of controls. He explained the instruments on the fascia panel, but said all we really needed to concern ourselves with were the altimeter and the speed indicator.

Before I got into the glider I'd noticed a short strand of wool stuck to the outside of the cockpit cover and being of a tidy mind, was tempted to pull it off. Just as well I didn't for he said to me later, 'Keep your eye on that strand of wool for depending what angle it is at, it will tell you how steeply we are banking, or if it's straight down the middle you'll know we are flying dead level.'

'Good Lord, I thought. So much for my tidy mind.

Having overcome my initial fear, I was just beginning to relax and enjoy the Experience, when the voice behind alarmed me by saying, 'Right. You've had your instructions, now I'm going to hand over to you. Have you remembered everything I've said?'

'Yes. Yes I have,' I eagerly assured him, for I did not wish to appear stupid.

'Right,' he said. 'it's all yours.'

'Really! You're joking!'

'Don't worry,' he said. 'If anything goes wrong I'll take over. The joystick is very responsive, so handle it with sensitivity. It will respond to the gentlest touch. Slightly incline it to the left if you want to go left; to the right if you want to go right; backward if you want to go up and forward to descend.'

'Are you sure you want to put your life in my hands?' I called back.

'You're doing fine,' he assured me. 'I feel a lot safer with you than I do with a lot of young men I give lessons to. They're much too heavy handed on the joy stick.'

Cheered by his encouraging words, I was now beginning to really enjoy myself as we danced the skies in effortless, noiseless flight. We wheeled and swung, then climbed sunward and topped the windswept hills. I looked down on the patchwork of fields and forest, criss-crossed by lanes and dotted here and there with farms and cottages. I was told that if I looked into the far distance I could see the Bristol Channel, that the blur beyond was the North Devon coast. The Malvern Hills were to be seen in another direction and the hills of Shropshire were visible to my left.

All too soon my time was up and the instructor took over the controls. We flew high in the sunlit silence, banked and circled a few times, then, with easy grace, gently glided to earth.

Joan didn't have much to say about her birthday escapade. Enough that she'd had the courage to do it and had induced me to join her. As for me, it was probably one of the most exhilarating experiences of my very long life and one I shall cherish for what is left of it.

Joan is now a very frail lady and we haven't been on any more mad escapades. It wasn't just an aerial fling we had together but our final fling.

At the ripe old age of eighty six I also decided it was time I retired from the Kington Choral Society, where I'd been singing since I was in my mid-seventies. My decision was precipitated when the friend I always stood next to, who had a very keen ear, told me I was flat, which was quite a strange thing to say since I wasn't actually singing at the time. Perhaps it was her way of saying I was past it, but all good things must come to an end and I was grateful I'd had the opportunity of performing so many well known choral works and some not so well known. Even if I wasn't singing flat, I always *felt* a bit flat when a performance was over and the fleeting sense of euphoria had deserted me. So many weeks of rehearsal and then it would all be over in a flash. I will be forever grateful to my friend Maureen Twiddy – the Musical Director – for affording me some of the happiest times of my declining years.

Chapter 61

My 90th Birthday

After surviving a heart attack the previous year and coping with a few other minor age related health problems, thanks to the marvels of modern medicine I am once more fit and functional and was able to happily celebrate my 90th birthday on November 7th 2013. And what a happy birthday week it was. It started with a birthday lunch at my favourite eating establishment with five of my most favourite people. A few days later, although I was now no longer singing regularly, I was unable to pass up the opportunity to sing in a charity performance of Faure's Requiem, making the week of celebrations even more special.

On the Sunday, it being Remembrance Day, I dressed suitably to match the solemnity of the occasion and went to church, proudly wearing my two war medals on the left breast of my jacket. To mark the occasion, I asked my friend Clare to take my photograph thus attired, so that I could keep it as a sort of souvenir of survival.

I then changed into less severe clothes to look my best for the celebrations still to come.

Due to work commitments, niece Susan hadn't been able to see me on my birthday but said she, husband Geoffrey and nephew Christopher, would come over on the Sunday afternoon to take me out for tea. Clare knew the venue, but no one would tell me where it was and I thought we would be going to some posh hotel in the countryside that specialises in these things. So I was surprised when we fetched up at a place not a mile from my home and wondered why it had been kept such a guarded secret. I soon found out. When I entered the venue, which I later learned had been hired for the occasion, I was shocked to see the place heaving with people; balloons and bunting festooning the ceiling; the tables groaning with goodies, and an impressive birthday cake (made by Susan) dominating one table, with a huge collage, made by great niece Katie, displaying, it seemed, almost every photograph of me that had ever been taken. There were friends from near and far, and relations from far and wide, all singing a hearty rendition of Happy Birthday, whilst I stood, smiling and blinking with astonishment.

When it was all over, tired but happy, I eased myself into bed, and before sleep engulfed me, reflected: How privileged am I, at the age of ninety to have just finished celebrating one of the happiest birthdays of my life.

And I thought, as I have thought so many times in the past: whatever misfortune may have befallen me in my early years – life has made it up to me a thousandfold since.

After all - A Life is What You Get – and we have to make the best we can of it.

THE END

.